KB054852

주한미군지위협정(SOFA)

군민관계
임시분과위원회 5

주한미군지위협정(SOFA)

군민관계
임시분과위원회 5

한국학술정보

| 머리말

　미국은 오래전부터 우리나라 외교에 있어서 가장 긴밀하고 실질적인 우호·협력관계를 맺어 온 나라다. 6·25전쟁 정전 협정이 체결된 후 북한의 재침을 막기 위한 대책으로서 1953년 11월 한미 상호방위조약이 체결되었다. 이는 미군이 한국에 주둔하는 법적 근거였고, 그렇게 주둔하게 된 미군의 시설, 구역, 사업, 용역, 출입국, 통관과 관세, 재판권 등 포괄적인 법적 지위를 규정하는 것이 바로 주한미군지위협정(SOFA)이다. 그러나 이와 관련한 협상은 계속된 난항을 겪으며 한미 상호방위조약이 체결로부터 10년이 훌쩍 넘은 1967년이 돼서야 정식 발효에 이를 수 있었다. 그럼에도 당시 미군 범죄에 대한 한국의 재판권은 심한 제약을 받았으며, 1980년대 후반 민주화 운동과 함께 미군 범죄 문제가 사회적 이슈로 떠오르자 협정을 개정해야 한다는 목소리가 커지게 되었다. 이에 1991년 2월 주한미군지위협정 1차 개정이 진행되었고, 이후에도 여러 사건이 발생하며 2001년 4월 2차 개정이 진행되어 현재에 이르고 있다.

　본 총서는 외교부에서 작성하여 최근 공개한 주한미군지위협정(SOFA) 관련 자료를 담고 있다. 1953년 한미 상호방위조약 체결 이후부터 1967년 발효가 이뤄지기까지의 자료와 더불어, 이후 한미 합동위원회을 비롯해 민·형사재판권, 시설, 노무, 교통 등 각 분과위원회의 회의록과 운영 자료, 한국인 고용인 문제와 관련한 자료, 기타 관련 분쟁 자료 등을 포함해 총 42권으로 구성되었다. 전체 분량은 약 2만 2천여 쪽에 이른다.

2024년 3월

한국학술정보(주)

| 일러두기

· 본 총서에 실린 자료는 2022년 4월과 2023년 4월에 각각 공개한 외교문서 4,827권, 76만 여 쪽 가운데 일부를 발췌한 것이다.

· 각 권의 제목과 순서는 공개된 원본을 최대한 반영하였으나, 주제에 따라 일부는 적절히 변경하였다.

· 원본 자료는 A4 판형에 맞게 축소하거나 원본 비율을 유지한 채 A4 페이지 안에 삽입 하였다. 또한 현재 시점에선 공개되지 않아 '공란'이란 표기만 있는 페이지 역시 그대로 실었다.

· 외교부가 공개한 문서 각 권의 첫 페이지에는 '정리 보존 문서 목록'이란 이름으로 기록물 종류, 일자, 명칭, 간단한 내용 등의 정보가 수록되어 있으며, 이를 기준으로 0001번부터 번호가 매겨져 있다. 이는 삭제하지 않고 총서에 그대로 수록하였다.

· 보고서 내용에 관한 더 자세한 정보가 필요하다면, 외교부가 온라인상에 제공하는 『대한 민국 외교사료요약집』 1991년과 1992년 자료를 참조할 수 있다.

| 차례

		정 리 보 존 문 서 목 록				

기록물종류	일반공문서철	등록번호	512	등록일자	
분류번호	729.419	국가코드		보존기간	영구
명 칭	SOFA 한.미국 합동위원회 군민관계 임시분과위원회, 제16-24차. 1973				
생 산 과	안보담당관실	생산년도	1973-1973	담당그룹	북미국
권 차 명					
내용목차	1. 제16차. 1973.1.12 2. 제17차. 1973.2.26 3. 제18차. 1973.3.16 4. 제19차. 1973.5.18 5. 제20차. 1973.6.15 6. 제21차. 1973.7.20 7. 제22차. 1973.9.25 8. 제23차. 1973.10.30 9. 제24차. 1973.12.7				

결 번

넘버링 오류

결 번

넘버링 오류

1. 제 16 차
   1973. 1. 12

4

기 안 용 지

분류기호 문서번호	미이 723 -	(전화번호)	전결규정 조 항 국장 전결사항
처리기간			
시행일자	1973. 1. 9.		
보존년한			국 장

보 조 기 관	과 장	9ℓ		협 조	
기안책임자	권 찬	북미2과			

| 경
유
수 신
참 조 | 수신처 참조 | 발
신 | 발 499
1973 1 9 | 통 | 1973 1 9 |
| 제 목 | SOFA 군민관계 분과위 제 16차 회의 개최 | | | | |

1. 한미 군대지위협정에 의한 한미 합동위원회 군민관계 분위 제 16차
   회의를 73. 1. 12. 15:30 외무부 회의실에서 개최키로 되었아오니
   각 위원들은 필히 참석하여 주시기 바랍니다.

2. 각 위원들은 감독부처가 집행중에 있는 기지촌시책 현황의 진척도를
   준비, 동회의에서 보고하여 주시기 바랍니다. 끝.

수신처 : 내무부장관 (지방국장, 치안국장)	정서
법무부장관 (검찰국장)	
고통부장관, 보건사획부장관, 문학공보부장관	관인
청와대 정무수석비서관 (내무, 보사담당 비서관)	
	발송

회의 참석 보고

1. 회의명 : SOFA 군민관계분위 제16차 한미 합동회의
2. 일시 : 73. 1. 12. 15:30 -
3. 장소 : 외무부 회의실
4. 참석자 : 김기조 북미 2과장

    권 찬 북미 2과

첨부 : Tentative Agenda.

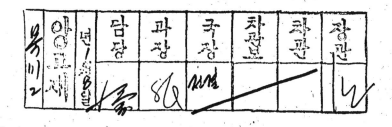

TENTATIVE

AGENDA OF SIXTEENTH MEETING
AD HOC SUBCOMMITTEE ON CIVIL-MILITARY RELATIONS
1530 HOURS, 12 JANUARY 1973, ROK CAPITOL BUILDING

I.   Status Reports on the Implementation of Subcommittee Recommendations - US and ROK Presentations.

II.   Plans for Future Ad Hoc Subcommittee Trips:

    1. Proposed Trip to Uijongbu - Friday, 26 January.

    2. Proposed Trip to Pyongtaek-gun (Camp Humphreys-Anjong-ni and Osan Air Base-Songtan-eup) - Friday, 2 February.

    3. Proposed Trip to Camp Casey - Tongduchon - 23 February.

III. Proposed Time for the Seventeenth Ad Hoc Subcommittee Meeting 1530 Hours, Tuesday, 20 February 1973 - US SOFA Conference Room.

IV.   Adjourn.

7

공   란

공   란

공 란

공   란

공　　란

공   란

공　　　란

공　　　란

공   란

공   란

공　　　란

공   란

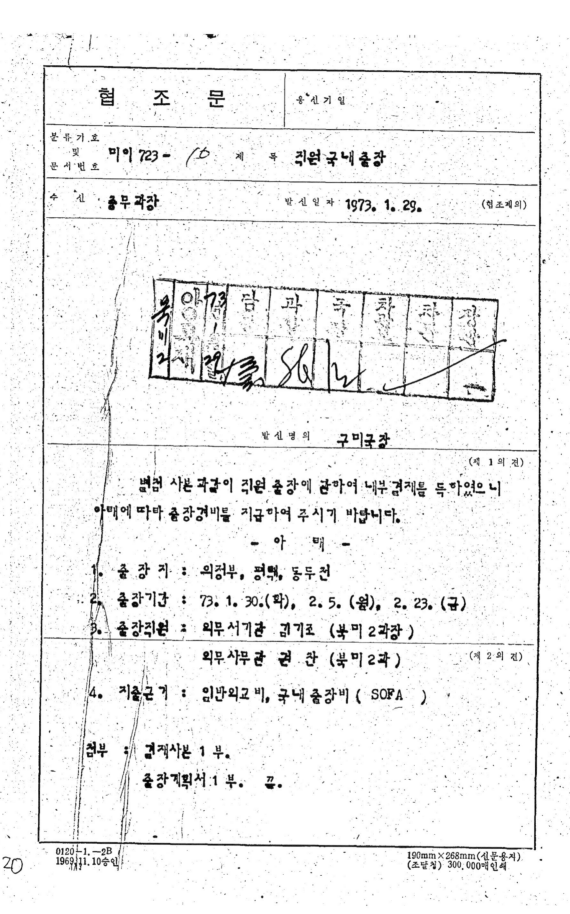

| 협 조 문 | 응신기일 | |

분류기호
및
문서번호　미이 723 - /0　제 목　직원국내출장

수 신　총무과장　　　발신일자　1973. 1. 29.　（협조제의）

발신명의　구미국장

（제 1 의 견）

　별첨 사본과같이 직원 출장에 관하여 내부결재를 득하었으니
아래에따라 출장경비를 지급하여 주시기 바랍니다.

- 아　래 -

1. 출 장 지 : 의정부, 평택, 동두천
2. 출장기간 : 73. 1. 30.(화), 2. 5. (월), 2. 23. (금)
3. 출장직원 : 외무서기관 김기조 (북미2과장)
　　　　　　 외무사무관 권 찬 (북미2과)　（제 2 의 견）

4. 지출근거 : 일반외교비, 국내출장비 (SOFA)

첨부 : 결재사본 1 부.
　　　출장계획서 1 부.　끝.

0120-1.-2B
1969.11.10승인

190mm×268mm(신문용지)
(조달청) 300,000매인쇄

20

출 장 기 획

1. 목 적 지 : 의정부, 평택, 동두천

2. 출장일정 : 73. 1. 29. 서울 출발 - 의정부 도착 (버스)

                1. 30. 의정부출발 - 서울 도착 (")

                2. 4. 서울 출발 - 평택 도착 (")

                2. 5. 평택 출발 - 서울 도착 (")

                2. 22. 서울 출발 - 동두천도착 (")

                2. 23. 동두천출발 - 서울 도착 (")

21

기 안 용 지

분류기호 문서번호	미이 723 -	(전화번호)	전결규정 조 항 **차 관** 전결사항
처 리 기 간			
시 행 일 자	1973. 1. 12.		
보 존 년 한			차 관

보 조 기 관	차관보		협	
	국 장			
	과 장		조	
기 안 책 임 자	권 찬 북미2과			

경 유		발		통	
수 신	내부결재				
참 조		신		제	

제 목 : 지원 출장

　　　한.미 군대지위협정에 의한 한.미 합동위원회는 주한미군 주둔지역
기지주변에서의 한국 민간인과 주둔 미군과의 관계개선을 도울 목적으로
72년 9월에 그 산하에 군.민관계 분과위원회를 설치하여 그동안 활동하여
왔는바, 미측은 동 분과위원회 활동의 일환으로 아래의 미군 기지들을
한.미 합동으로 시찰하여 대책을 건의할것을 제의하여 왔아옵기, 아래와
같이 출장시킬것을 건의합니다.

　　　　　　　　　　　　　- 아 래 -

1. 출장직원 : 김기조 북미2과장 (동분과위 한국측 의장)

　　　　　　　권 찬 북미2과 (동분과위 간사)

2. 출장지 : (1) 1. 30. (화) : 의정부 한.미 제1 혼성군단 사령부

　　　　　　(2) 2. 5. (월) : 평택 미 23지원단 (Camp

　　　　　　　　　　Humphreys) 및 오산 공군기지

　　　　　　(3) 2. 23. (금) : 동두천 미 제2사단 (Camp

　　　　　　　　　　Casey)　끝.

결 번

넘버링 오류

결 번

넘버링 오류

결 번

넘버링 오류

결 번

넘버링 오류

2. 제17차

1973. 2. 26

27

기 안 용 지

분류기호 문서번호	미이 723 -	(전화번호　　　　)	전 결 규 정 조 항 국장　　전 결 사 항	
처 리 기 간				
시 행 일 자	1973. 2. 20.		*8ᄂ*대	
보 존 년 한			국　　　　장	

보 조 기 관	과　　장	*8ᄂ*		협	
				조	
기 안 책 임 자	변승국	북미 2 과			

경　유					발		통	
수　신 참　조	수신처 참조						제	
제　목	SOFA 군민관계 분과위 제 17차 회의 개최							

한.미 군대지위협정에 의한 한.미 합동위원회 군민관계 분과위

제17차 회의를 73. 2. 26. 15:30 미8군 SOFA 회의실에서

개최키로 되었아오니 각 위원들은 필히 참석하여 주시기 바랍니다. 끔.

수신처 :　내무부장관 (지방국장, 치안국장)

　　　　　법무부장관 (검찰국장)

　　　　　교통부장관 , 보건사회부장관, 문학공보부장관

　　　　　대통령 정무수석 비서관 (내무. 보사담당 비서관)

	정 서
	관 인
	발 송

건의사항

1973. 2. 23

1 성병 퇴치를 위한 건의

(1) 영내크라브에 특수 연예부(윤락여성) 출입제한

영내크라브에 특수 연예부가 매일 200 명 이상이 출입함으로서

A. 전염병을 유발케하고 미 검진자의 도피처로 되고있다

B. 전염병 예방 질서를 파괴한다

C. 사병교육을 강화할것 (미 검진자 및 노상 접객등에 응하지 못하도록)

2. 대한민족 배을 존속하기위한 건의

(1) 부대측에 지나친 간섭지양

A. 연대장이 사병에게 명령하듯 부대측이 간섭이 심하다

B. 일방적으로 암행 검열을 하고 결과가 불량하다는 이유로 업소에 미군출입 금지 조치를 하여 주민들에게 크게 위협을 주고 있다

C. 카운타 뷔적 빠스등을 샅샅이 뒤지고 복장·명찰·청소 부록까지 지시하는등 간섭이 심하다

D. 흑 백 인에 싸움을 우리에게 책임이 있는양 전가함은 부당하다 (음악이 고르지 않다、흑인과 춤을 추지 않는다는 등)

3. 검열、미군 출입금지 조치등은 한측 기관에 의해서 만이 가능해야 한다

관광 휴양 업자들의 결의사항

(1) 제 1 항이 시정되지 않으면 성병 퇴치가 불능함으로 특수 연예부를 고용(기생)치 않고 위 문제는 만일 고용 음료수 판매 사업 만을 하겠다 (단 특수 연예부의 해결문제는 한국이 책임져야 한다)

(2) 제 2 항이 관철되지 않으면 비한측의 엄연한 내정 간섭 임으로 관철 될때까지 산하 22 개 관광 휴양업소는 자진 폐업법 절서가 회복 될때까지 폭쟁한다

한국관광 휴양업 협회 양주지부

29

7 members

RBK   _superintendent Lee Myung Mo._

미국인 강제퇴거자 명단

1972. 6 - 1973. 2.

성 명	생년월일	입국목적	출입국상황		퇴거일자	퇴거 사유
			입국	출국		
███████	48. 3. 22.	관광	71.9. 15.	72.3. 14.	72. 6.29	불법 체류 _illegal stay_
	49. 6. 3.	휴가	71.8. 12.	72.7. 1.	72. 3.24.	습관성의약품관리법위반으로징역1년복역중, 가석방.
	48. 7. 13.		72.6. 11.		72. 7.15.	_Violation of drug control law_ 한국에서제대한자로서군인으로가장입국 _Illegal Re-entry_ (밀입국)
	47. 6. 7.	관광	69.12. 22.		72. 7. 4.	불법 체류
	47. 8. 16.	관광	71.10. 4.		72. 11.11	불법체류 _Korean violation narcotics law._
	52. 7. 18.	관광	72.5. 22.		72. 11.23	마약법위반으로징역6월복역후석방.
	48. 12.12.				73. 2. 3.	입국사증없이 _without_ 입국(밀입국). _Visa_

30

공   란

공   란

공   란

공   란

공 란

공 란

공 란

공　　　란

공 란

공   란

공   란

공　　　란

공   란

공   란

주한미군지위협정(SOFA) 군민관계 임시분과위원회 5

공   란

공   란

공   란

공   란

93d Congress }
1st Session }

COMMITTEE PRINT

THE U.S. HEROIN PROBLEM AND SOUTHEAST ASIA

REPORT

OF A

STAFF SURVEY TEAM

OF THE

COMMITTEE ON FOREIGN AFFAIRS
HOUSE OF REPRESENTATIVES

JANUARY 11, 1973

Printed for the use of the Committee on Foreign Affairs

U.S. GOVERNMENT PRINTING OFFICE

86-565
WASHINGTON : 1973

UNITED STATES ANTIDRUG EFFORT IN JAPAN

Unlike the U.S. Missions' narcotics programs in Laos, Thailand, and South Vietnam, the U.S. Embassy in Toyko does not appear to regard the effort against narcotics as one of high priority in Japan. Although BNDD and Customs have personnel incountry attached to the U.S. Mission, there is little, if any, overall coordination of the narcotics program.

Whereas the Ambassador is directly involved in the narcotics programs in the U.S. Missions in Southeast Asia, the U.S. Ambassador to Japan has no visible role on the Mission's narcotics committee where he is represented by a low-ranking foreign service officer who must meet with intelligence and enforcement officials with much more rank and experience.

KOREA

In addition to covering narcotics activities in Japan, one of the BNDD agents assigned to the U.S. Embassy in Tokyo monitors drug activity in South Korea on a temporary duty (TDY) basis. According to the agent, the U.S. military population in Korea, which totals approximately 40,000, is vulnerable to drug abuse.

In support of his evaluation, he cited figures which show the results of 47,492 urinalysis tests taken as of May 31, 1972. Among those tested, 1,811 were positive and 689 hospitalized for detoxification. Withdrawal symptoms were observable in 206 of those hospitalized. Of that latter figure, 85 were found to be on barbiturates, 5.8 percent on amphetamines, 8.8 percent on opiates including methadone, morphine, and heroin.

According to two military doctors who work with drug users in Korea, 20 to 30 percent of all GI's under 25 use barbiturates while some 200 military personnel per month voluntarily request help to shake drug dependence.

In terms of availability, the area surrounding U.S. military bases is called a "no-man's land" where drugs are easy to purchase. Enforcement is minimal since there is no domestic coordination by the Korean police against trafficking. Moreover, the United States does not yet have a country plan devised for Korea. The agent who covers the area on a part-time basis is currently assimilating the information necessary to devise such a plan.

50

Inclosure 2

3. 제 18 차

   1973. 3. 16

'51

MONTHLY STATISTICAL REPORT OF CONSTRUCTION CONTRACTS & EARNINGS

MAR. 1973

Prepared By

KOREA MILITARY CONSTRUCTION CONTRACTORS ASSOCIATION

Rm 303, 3rd Floor, Kyonggi Bldg.
115, SAMKAK-DONG, CHUNG-KU,
SEOUL, KOREA
TEL. 23-1475, 23-1476, 28-4033

CONTENTS

* This report is prepared on the basis of "Date information received" irrespective of actual contract date.

* The statistics contained in this report cover only Domestic figures since January 1, 1971.

SUMMARY OF CONTRACTS & EARNINGS

MONTH	CONTRACTS		EARNINGS ($)
	NUMBERS	AMOUNTS ($)	
JANUARY	17	681,686.53	1,573,139.31
FEBRUARY	10	852,590.33	913,350.34
MARCH	19	371,220.03	971,993.39
TOTAL	46	1,905,496.89	3,458,483.04

54

CONTRACTS & EARNINGS BY THE PROCUREMENT AGENCIES

PROCUREMENT AGENCY	CONTRACTS				EARNINGS	
	MAR. 1973		ACCUMULATED TOTAL(JAN-MAR)		MAR. 1973 ($)	ACCUMULATED TOTAL(JAN-MAR) ($)
	NO. OF CONTR.	AMOUNT($)	NO. OF CONTR.	AMOUNT($)		
US ARMY KPA	8	43,254.23	16	142,104.58	174,230.18	400,505.57
US ARMY EDFE	1	296,655.86	4	1,253,841.18	555,045.56	2,257,150.50
USAF KPC	0	-26,010.29	12	443,276.31	235,688.06	669,753.27
OTHERS	10	57,320.23	14	66,274.82	7,029.59	131,073.70
TOTAL	19	371,220.03	46	1,905,496.89	971,993.32	3,458,483.04

CONTRACTS & EARNINGS BY CATEGORIES

TYPE OF CONSTRUCTION	CONTRACTS		EARNINGS	
	MAR. 1972 ($)	ACCUMULATED TOTAL(JAN-MAR) ($)	MAR. 1972 ($)	ACCUMULATED TOTAL(JAN-MAR) ($)
BRIDGE WORK, STEEL	0	0	0	0
CIVIL ENGINEERING	0	-2,348.14	169,812.06	326,216.46
CONST., BUILDING	376,163.26	1,351,645.20	748,574.93	2,928,470.14
CONST., HARBOR	0	0	0	0
CONST., RAILROAD	0	0	0	0
CONST., ROAD PAVING & REPAIR	-20,370.23	248,616.15	1,667.02	126,368.13
ELECTRICAL WORKS	0	292,821.93	33,228.86	56,727.58
INSTALLATION OF COMMUNICATIONS	15,427.00	14,761.75	18,710.52	20,700.73
TOTAL	371,220.03	1,905,496.89	971,993.39	3,458,483.04

56

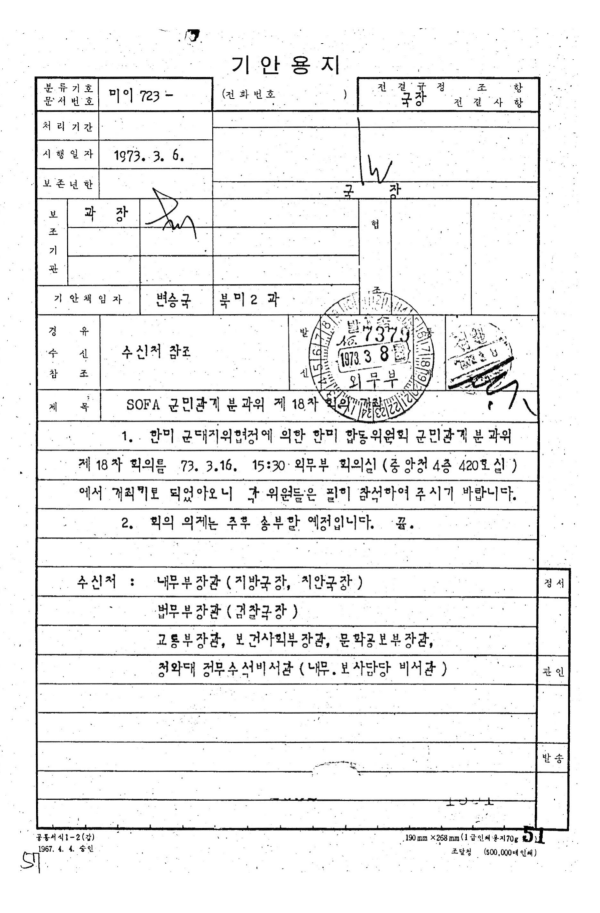

기 안 용 지

분류기호 문서번호	미이 723 -	(전화번호)	전 결 규 정 조 항 국장 전 결 사 항
처 리 기 간			
시 행 일 자	1973. 3. 6.		
보 존 년 한			국 장
보 조 기 관	과 장		협
기 안 책 임 자	변승국	북 미 2 과	조
경 유 수 신 참 조	수신처 참조	발 신	
제 목	SOFA 군민관계 분과위 제 18차 회의 개최		

1. 한미 군대지위협정에 의한 한미 합동위원회 군민관계 분과위

제 18차 회의를 73. 3. 16. 15:30 외무부 회의실 (중앙청 4층 420호실)

에서 개최키로 되었아오니 각 위원들은 필히 참석하여 주시기 바랍니다.

2. 회의 의제는 추후 송부할 예정입니다. 끝.

수신처 :   내무부장관 (지방국장, 치안국장)

법무부장관 (검찰국장)

교통부장관, 보건사회부장관, 문화공보부장관,

청와대 정무수석비서관 (내무. 보사담당 비서관)

| | 정서 |
| 관인 |
| 발송 |

기 안 용 지

분류기호 문서번호	미이 723 -	(전화번호)	전결규정 조항	
			국장	전결사항
처 리 기 간				
시 행 일 자	1973. 3. 12.			
보 존 년 한			국 장	
보조기관	과 장		협	
기 안 책 임 자	김성실 북미2과			
경 유 수 신 참 조	수신처 참조	발 신	1973.3.12	
제 목	SOFA 군민관계 임시분과위원회 회의 의제송부			

1973. 3. 16. (금) 15:30 시에 한국 중앙청 (외무부 회의실) 서관 507A 회의실

에서 개최될 군민관계 임시분과위원회 제18차 회의 의제를 별첨

송부하오니, 회의 토의자료를 준비하시기 바랍니다.

첨부 : 군민관계 임시분과위원회 제18차회의 의제 1부. 끝.

	정서
수신처 : 내무부 (치안국, 지방국장) 법무부 (검찰국장)(법무실장)	
보사부 (만성병 담당관) 교통부 (관광국장)	관인
문공부 (해외 공보관장)	
	발송

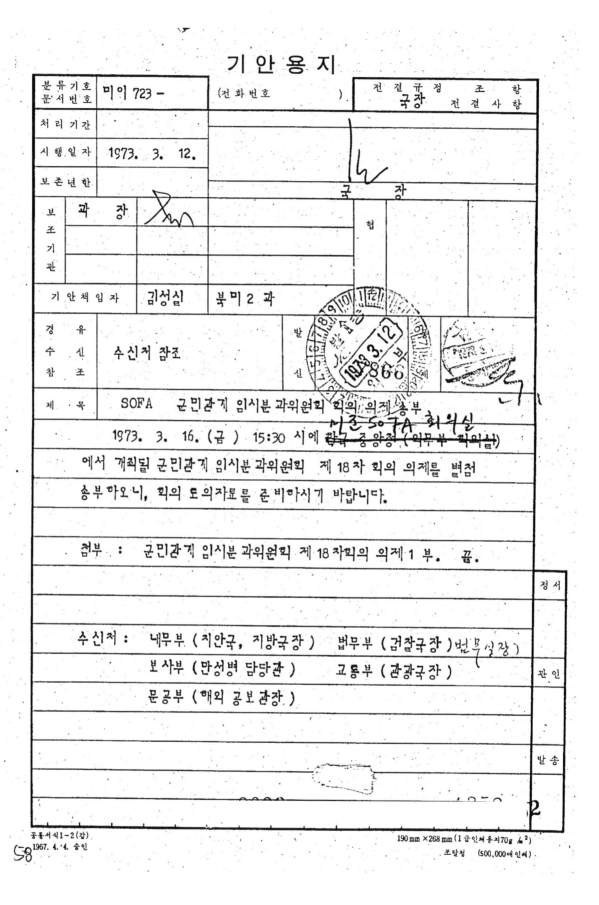

공   란

공   란

주한미군지위협정(SOFA) 군민관계 임시분과위원회 5

공   란

공   란

공 란

공 란

공   란

공　　　　란

공   란

공 란

공　　　란

공   란

공　　란

공   란

주한미군지위협정(SOFA) 군민관계 임시분과위원회 5

공　　　　란

공 란

공   란

공   란

공　　　란

4. 제19차.

1973. 5. 18.

78

기 안 용 지

분류기호 문서번호	미이 723 -		(전화번호)		전결규정 9 조 2 항 국장 전결사항	
처 리 기 간						
시 행 일 자	1973. 4. 19.				국 장	
보 존 년 한						
보 조 기 관	과 장			협		
				조		
기 안 책 임 자	양세훈	북미 2 과				
경 유 수 신 참 조	수신처 참조		발 신	13269 발송	통 제	검열 1973.4.19
제 목	SOFA 군민관계 분과위원회 회의 취소			1973. 4. 19		

1. 73. 4. 20. 개최 예정이던 한미 SOFA 군민관계 분과위
회의가 정부 을지연습 실시 관계로 취소되었음을 알려드리오니 양지
하시기 바랍니다.

2. 차기 회의 개최 일자등에 관하여는 추후 통보 위계입니다.

끝.

수신처 : 내무부장관 (지방국장, 치안국장)	정서
법무부장관 (법무실장, 검찰국장, 출입국관리국장)	관인
보건사회부장관 (보건국장)	
교통부장관 (관광국장)	
문학공보부장관 (공보국장)	발송
청와대 정무수석 비서관 (내무.보사담당 비서관)	

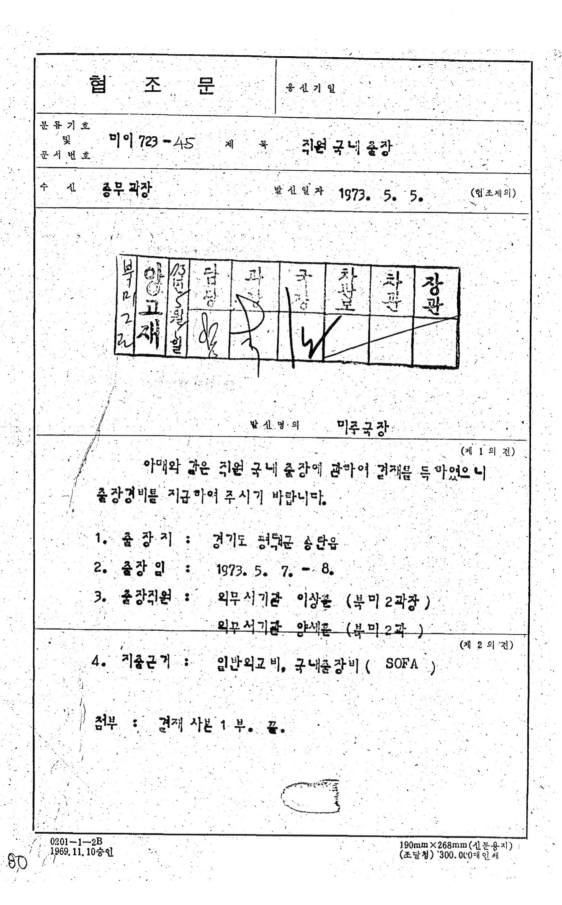

협 조 문	용신기일

| 분류기호 및 문서번호 | 미이 723-45 | 제 목 | 직원 국내출장 |

| 수 신 | 총무과장 | 발신일자 1973. 5. 5. | (협조제의) |

발신명의   미주국장

(제 1 의 견)

아래와 같은 직원 국내출장에 관하여 결재를 득 하였으니 출장경비를 지급하여 주시기 바랍니다.

1. 출 장 지 :   경기도 평덕군 송탄읍

2. 출 장 일 :   1973. 5. 7. ~ 8.

3. 출장직원 :   외무서기관 이상훈 (북미 2과장)

　　　　　　　　 외무서기관 양세훈 (북미 2과)

(제 2 의 견)

4. 지출근거 :   일반외교비, 국내출장비 (SOFA)

첨부 :   결재 사본 1부. 끝.

0201-1-2B
1969. 11. 10승인

190mm×268mm (신문용지)
(조달청) '300.000매 인 쇄

기 안 용 지

분류기호 문서번호	미이 723 -	(전 화 번 호)	전 결 규 정 조 항 차관 전 결 사 항
처 리 기 간			
시 행 일 자	1973. 5. 5.		차 관
보 존 년 한			

보조기관	차관보		협조	
	국 장			동부리장.
	과 장			
기 안 책 임 자	양세훈 북미 2 과			

경유 수신 참조	내부결재	발 신		통 제	
제 목	직원 출장				

최근 송탄읍 소재 미군기지 주변에서 발생한 폭행사건 및 미군

당국의 일부지역 출입금지 조치등 기지촌에서의 불상사와 관련하여,

SOFA 군민관계 분과위원회 미국측 의장은 사실조사 및 대책강구를

위한 긴급 현지답사 실시를 제의하여 왔으므로, 아래와 같이 관계직원을

출장시킬것을 건의합니다.

		정서
1. 출장직원 : 이상훈 북미 2과장 (동 분위 한국측 의장) 양세훈 서기관 (동 분위 간사)		
2. 출장일시 : 1973. 5. 7. (월) - 8. (화)		
3. 출장지 : 경기도 평택군 송탄읍		관인

참고 : 동 분과위원회는 현재까지 총 20회에 걸쳐 기지촌 시찰을
       실시한바 있으며, 한국측으로서는 관계부처 관계위원 및
       현지 관계관들이 참석하여 왔음.
		발송

공동서식1-2(갑)
1967. 4. 4. 승인

190 mm ×268 mm (1급인쇄용지70g ㎡)
조달청 (500,000매 인쇄)

참 고 사 항

1. 5. 2. 송탄읍의 관광업소 클럽에서 한국인에 의하여 미 공군
    헌병이 복부 자상, 현 한미 합동으로 조사 진행중.

2. 미군당국은 30일간 미군인의 일부지역 출입금지 조치 및 차후
    전지역 금지조치 경고.

3. 오산기지 주둔 미군당국 서한에서 제시된 문제점

    (1) 과거 수 개월간 미군인에 대한 수많은 폭행사건 및 범죄
         행위 발생

    (2) 가로등 시설 불충분

    (3) 수 차 통고에도 불구하고 보안등 정비불량

    (4) 관광업소의 고객 안전 조치 전무

    (5) 송탄읍 주민 5만에 비하여 한국 경찰 병력 소수 배치

    (6) 미군인에 대한 보호 조치 촉구하였으나 만족한 조치 전무

    (7) 경찰당국의 실시사항 통보 요망

한.미 합동 기지촌 시찰

1.	1971. 9. 10.	동두천	Camp Casey
2.	1971. 9. 13.	평택군 안정리	Camp Humphreys
3.	1971. 9. 24.	평택군 송탄읍	Osan Air Base
4.	1971. 9. 28.	대구	Camp Henry Walker
5.	1971. 9. 30.	부평	ASCOM
6.	1971. 10. 7.	군산	Kunsan Air Base
7.	1971. 10. 28.	이태원, 용산	
8.	1971. 11. 14. - 15.	부산	Hialeah Compound
9.	1971. 11. 30.	파주군	
10.	1971. 12. 3.	대전	Camp Ames
11.	1972. 2. 25.	평택군 안정리	Camp Humphreys
12.	1972. 3. 30.	동두천	Camp Casey
13.	1972. 5. 1.	부평	ASCOM
14.	1972. 5. 10.	춘천	Camp Page
15.	1972. 6. 2.	왜관	Camp Carroll
16.	1972. 6. 9.	진해, 마산	44th Eng Bn
17.	1973. 1. 30.	의정부	
18.	1973. 2. 5.	평택	Camp Humphreys
19.	1973. 2. 5.	송탄읍	Osan Air Base
20.	1973. 2. 23.	동두천	Camp Casey
21.	1973. 3. 22.	이태원, 용산	
22.	1973. 5. 7.	평택군 송탄읍	Osan Air Base

기 안 용 지

분류기호 문서번호	미이 723 -	(전 화 번 호　　　　)	전결규정 **9**조**2**항 국장　전결사항

처 리 기 간		
시 행 일 자	1973. 5. 9.	
보 존 년 한		

보 조 기 관	과 장		협 조	
기안책임자	양세훈	북미2과		

경 유		통	
수 신	수신처 참조		
참 조		제	

발 16165
273.5 10

제　목　SOFA 군민관계 분과위원회 제19차 회의 개최

한미 군대지위협정에 의한 한미 합동위원회 군민관계 임시분과

위원회 제19차 회의가 별첨과 같이 73. 5. 18. 15:30 외무부 회의실

(중앙청 4층 420호실)에서 개최되오니 각 위원들은 필히 참석하여

주시기 바랍니다.　　　　이에따라하시오

첨부 : ▩ 의제 1부.　끝.

수신처 : 내무부장관 (지방국장, 치안국장 (외사과, 수사지도과))

법무부장관 (법무실장, 검찰국장)

보건사회부장관 (보건국장)

교통부장관 (관광국장)

문화공보부장관 (공보국장)

청와대 정무수석비서관 (내무·보사담당 비서관)

정서
관인
발송

1378

공동서식1-2(갑)
1967. 4. 4. 승인　　　　　　　　190mm×268mm (1급인쇄용지70g /㎡)
조달청 (500,000매)

AGENDA OF NINETEENTH MEETING
AD HOC SUBCOMMITTEE ON CIVIL-MILITARY RELATIONS
1530 HOURS, 18 MAY 1973, ROK CAPITOL BUILDING

I.   Introduction of New Members - ROK Presentation.

II. Status Reports on the Implementation of
     Subcommittee Recommendations - ROK and US
     Presentations.

III. Discussion of the situation in the Osan-
     Songtan-eup area - US and ROK Presentations.

IV. Consideration of the Fourteenth Report of
     the Ad Hoc Subcommittee to the Joint Committee -
     ROK and US Presentations.

V.   Proposed Time for the Twentieth Ad Hoc Sub-
     committee Meeting, 1530 Hours, Friday, 15 June
     1973, US SOFA Conference Room.

VI. Adjourn.

85

기 안 용 지

분류기호 문서번호	미이 723 -	(전화번호)	전결규정 **9**조**2**항
			국장 전결사항

처리기간		
시행일자	**1973. 5. 11.**	
보존년한		

보조기관	과 장	(서명)		협 조	
			국 장		
기안책임자	양세훈	북미2과			

경유 수신 참조	수신처 참조	발 16366	통 1973.5.11.

제 목 : SOFA 군민관계분과위원회 제19차회의 대비(의제 제2항)

연 : 미이 723 - 16165 및 15463

1. SOFA 합동위 군민관계 분과위원회 제18차 회의
(73. 3. 16.)는 주지하시는 바와 같이 합동위원회에 대한 제13차
보고서를 채택하고, 그간 관계부처의 적극적 사업 추진으로 기지촌의
환경개선이 괄목할만한 성과를 이룩하였으나 아직도 성병, 마약 및
습관성 의약품, 재산도난 및 암거래등 분야에 있어서는 문제점이
지속되고 있어 이에 대한 한.미 공동 대책이 시급히 요청되고 있다고
보고하였읍니다.

2. 금반 동분과위 제19차 회의에서는 연호 (의제 제2항)로
알려드린바와 같이 상기 문제점들을 포함한 제반 사항에 대한 한.미
양측간의 토의가 있은후 제14차 보고서가 작성될 것이므로 귀부소관
사항에 관한 조치사항, 사업계획, 미측에 대한 요망등 아측이 제시할
사항을 준비하시어 금반 회의에 대비하여 주시기 바랍니다. 끝.

수신처 :　내무부장관 (지방국장, 치안국장 (외사과, 수사지도과))

법무부장관 (법무실장, 검찰국장)

보건사회부장관 (보건국장)

고용부장관 (관광국장)

문화공보부장관 (공보국장)

청와대 정무수석비서관 (내무.보사담당비서관)

'87

기 안 용 지

분류기호 문서번호	미이 723 -	(전화번호)	전결규정 9 조 2 항 국장 전결사항
처 리 기 간			
시 행 일 자	1973. 5. 11.		
보 존 년 한		국 장	

| 보
조
기
관 | 과 장 | | 협 | |
| 기 안 책 임 자 | 양세훈 북미2과 | | | |

경 유		
수 신	수신처 참조	통 제
참 조		

제 목 : SOFA 군민관계 분과위 제 19 차 회의 대비 (의제 제 3 항)

연 : 미이 723 - 15494 및 16165

1. SOFA 군민관계 분과위원회는 연호와 같이 송탄읍
사태로 인한 현지답사와 현지 관계관 및 미군당국을 포함한 한미
양측 간에 대책 강구를 위한 회합을 가졌읍니다.

2. 주지하시는 바와 같이 상기 회의에서 제기된 미측 요망
사항은 아래와 같사온바, 이중 일부는 관계부처의 신속한 조치로
이미 개선된 사항도 있으나, 금반 동분과위 제 19 차 회의에서 이에
대한 협의 (의제 제 3 항)가 될 예정이오니 귀부 소관사항에 관하여
아측 입장을 제시할수 있도록 대비하여 주시기 바랍니다.

가. 현지 경찰관 증원

나. 가로등 증설 및 보안등 정비 철저

다. 현 관광업소의 위치 이건

라. 관광업소 소재 주변의 도로망 정비

마. 관광업소 신규허가시의 위치등 환경조건 강화 및

정서

관인

발송

공통서식1-2(갑)
1967. 4. 4. 승인

190 mm ×268 mm (1 급인쇄용지70g ㎡)
조달청   (500,000매

신규허가 억제

바. 송탄읍의 시 승격에 의한 행정 강화   끝.

수신처 : 내무부장관 (지방국장 , 치안국장 (외사과, 수사지도과))

법무부장관 (법무실장, 검찰국장)

보건사회부장관 (보건국장)

교통부장관 (관광국장)

문화공보부장관 (공보국장)

청와대 정무수석비서관 (내무·보 사담당 비서관)

'39.

기 안 용 지

분류기호 문서번호	미이 723 -	(전화번호　　　)	전결규정 9 조 2 항
처 리 기 간			국장　　전 결 사 항
시 행 일 자	1973. 5. 14.		
보 존 년 한			국　～　장

보조기관	과　장		협
기안책임자	양세훈　북미 2 과		조
경 유			통
수 신	수신처 참조		제
참 조			
제 목	SOFA 군민관계 분과위원회 제 1 차 회의		

연 : 미이 723 - 15494 및 16567

연호 SOFA 군민관계 분과위원회의 송탄읍 현지답사시 미군

당국이 브리핑한 자료를 별첨 송부하오니 참고하시기 바랍니다.

✓ 첨부 : 자료 1통. 끝.

수신처 : 내무부장관(지방국장, 치안국장 (외사과, 수사지도과))

　　　　　　 법무부장관 (법무실장, 검찰국장)

　　　　　　 교통부장관 (관광국장)

　　　　　　 보건사회부장관 (보건국장)

　　　　　　 문화공보부장관 (공보국장)

　　　　　　 청와대 정무수석비서관 (내무.보사담당비서관)

1381

공동서식1-2(갑)
1967. 4. 4. 승인
190 mm × 268 mm (1 급 인쇄용지 70g ㎡)
조달청　(500,000 매 인쇄)

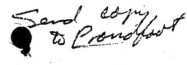

1. GOOD MORNING, GENTLEMEN. ON BEHALF OF THE 314TH AIR DIVISION AND THE

51ST AIR BASE WING, I'D LIKE TO WELCOME YOU ONCE AGAIN TO OSAN AIR BASE.

THE PURPOSE OF MY PRESENTATION THIS MORNING IS TO DISCUSS OUR MUTUAL

PROBLEM REGARDING SONGTAN-UP, OR AS IT IS KNOWN TO AMERICANS, CHICOL

VILLE. OVER THE PAST SEVERAL MONTHS WE HAVE BECOME INCREASINGLY CONCERNED

ABOUT THE NUMEROUS ASSAULTS AND OTHER FORMS OF VIOLENCE INVOLVING U.S.

FORCES PERSONNEL IN TOWN.

2. FIRST, PERMIT ME TO SET THE SCENE. THIS CHART DEPICTS THE NUMBER OF

SERIOUS ASSAULTS INVOLVING U.S. FORCES PERSONNEL WHICH HAVE OCCURRED IN

CHICOL VILLE SINCE JULY, 1972. AS YOU CAN SEE, WE HAVE A PROBLEM. ALMOST

50% INVOLVE KN'S, EITHER AS VICTIMS OR PERPETRATORS

3. HERE IS A MAP OF CHICOL VILLE INDICATING THE LOCATION OF THE TWELVE

CLUBS. AS YOU CAN SEE, MANY OF THEM ARE AWAY FROM THE MSR. (TALK TO ALLEYS -

TALK TO WESTERN VILLAGE.)

4. THIS NEXT CHART GIVES YOU AN INDICATION OF WHERE THESE INCIDENTS ARE

OCCURING. NOTE THAT OUR PROBLEM IS CONCENTRATED IN THE BACK ALLEYS LEADING

TO AND FROM THE CLUBS. (DISCUSS 33 NOT ON CHART IN VARIOUS COMPOUNDS, ETC.)

AT THIS POINT I WOULD LIKE TO GIVE YOU A BRIEF CHRONOLOGY OF EVENTS

LEADING TO OUR PRESENT SITUATION.

5. YOU MAY RECALL THAT ON NOVEMBER 2ND OF LAST YEAR, A DISTURBANCE

OCCURRED IN CHICOL VILLE INVOLVING AMERICAN SERVICEMEN AND KOREAN

NATIONALS. THIS LED TO A COUPLE OF MEETINGS THE NEXT DAY BETWEEN BASE

PERSONNEL, PREDOMINATLY BLACKS, AND BASE OFFICIALS, INCLUDING THE DIVISION

COMMANDER, GENERAL MCNEIL, IN WHICH MANY GRIEVANCES WERE AIRED. FOREMOST

AMOUNG THESE GRIEVANCES WERE CHARGES OF DISCRIMINATION AGAINST BLACKS AND

OTHER MINORITIES IN THE CLUBS IN CHICOL VILLE - - A DEFINITE CONTRIBUTING

FACTOR TO OUR ASSAULT RATE.

A MEETING WAS HELD WITH ALL THE CLUB OWNERS ON 10 NOVEMBER TO DISCUSS

THE PROBLEM AND TO SOLICIT THEIR COOPERATION IN ELIMINATING DISCRIMINATORY

PRACTICES. THIS SAME SUBJECT WAS DISCUSSED A FEW DAY EARLIER (NOVEMBER 8)

WITH MAJOR GENERAL BANG, WHO AT THE TIME WAS KYONGGI PROVINCE MARTIAL LAW

COMMANDER.

92

THE SITUATION IMPROVED SOMEWHAT AND ON JANUARY 16TH ANOTHER MEETING

WAS HELD WITH THE CLUB OWNERS TO REVIEW OUR PROGRESS. AT THAT TIME WE

STATED THAT IT WAS NOT OUR DESIRE TO PUT ANY CLUB OFF LIMITS, BUT THAT WE

WOULD HAVE NO ALTERNATIVE IF MORE DEFINITE PROGRESS TOWARD ELIMINATING

DISCRIMINATION AND CURBING VIOLENCE WAS NOT MADE.

THEN CAME FEBRUARY AND MARCH -- BAD MONTHS. A SERIES OF BRUTAL ASSAULTS

IN THE VARIOUS ALLEYS NEAR THE CLUBS PLUS DOCUMENTED CASES OF DISCRIMINATION

IN THE A-FRAME LEAD US TO TAKE A SERIES OF STEPS. WE HAD A PARTICULARLY BAD

WEEKEND, 9 - 11 FEBRUARY WHEN 4 ASSULTS OCCURED.

6. ON FEBRUARY 13TH A PROGRAM OF COURTESY PATROL TEAMS WAS INITIATED.

THESE WERE TEN TWO-MAN TEAMS COMPOSED OF OFFICERS AND SENIOR NCOs IN

UNIFORM. THEIR PURPOSE WAS TO CIRCULATE AMONG THE CLUBS AND IN THE VILLE

GENERALLY SO AS TO DETER ANY ACTS OF VIOLENCE. THE PROGRAM WAS ONLY

MODERATELY SUCCESSFUL. AT THE SAME TIME IT WAS ANNOUNCED TO OUR PEOPLE

THAT CONTINUATION OF THE ASSAULTS WOULD RESULT IN A REQUIREMENT FOR UNIFORMS

IN THE VILLAGE.

ALSO, IN MID-FEBRUARY WE SENT A LETTER TO SENIOR SUPERINTENDENT YUN,

CHIEF OF PYONGTAEK POLICE STATION, OUTLINING OUR PROBLEMS AND REQUESTING

93

HIS ASSISTANCE IM MAKING CHICOL VILLE SAFER. WE POINTED OUT THE NEED FOR

ADDITIONAL KOREAN NATIONAL POLICE AND MORE LIGHTING IN THE DARK ALLEYS.

SOME ADDITIONAL KNPs WERE ADDED AT THAT TIME. THESE STEPS PROVED PARTIALLY

SUCCESSFUL.

IN MID-MARCH THE A-FRAME WAS PLACED ON PROBATION FOR A PERIOD OF TEN

DAYS AS A RESULT OF DUCUMENTED DISCRIMINATORY PRACTICES. THEN, ON 30 MARCH

WE HAD A PARTICULARLY BRUTAL ASSAULT - - A G.I. WAS BEATEN WITH A CANE. AS

A CONSEQUENCE, SEVERAL ACTIONS WERE TAKEN: FIRST, SINCE THE SITUATION AT

THE A-FRAME HAD NOT IMPROVED SIGNIFICANTLY, IT WAS PLACED OFF LIMITS FOR A

PERIOD OF 15 DAYS. SECONDLY, WE FELT COMPELLED TO INSTITUTE A POLICY REQUIRING

THE WEAR OF THE UNIFORM IN CHICOL VILLE.

I MIGHT DIGRESS A MOMENT HERE TO STATE THAT THE UNIFORM POLICY HAS BEEN

WORKING VERY WELL. ALTHOUGH IT HAS UNDOUBTEDLY WORKED AN ECONOMIC HARDSHIP

ON THE COMMUNITY, IT HAS LED TO NUMBER OF POSITIVE RESULTS.

7. FIRST, IT HAS DECREASED THE NUMBER OF PEOPLE IN TOWN WHICH IS OVERCROWED

ALREADY AS IT IS. SECONDLY, ALL OUR PEOPLE ARE LOOKING BETTER AND BEHAVING

BETTER AS A CONSEQUENCE OF THE UNIFORM POLICY. AND FINALLY, WE HAVE FOUND

THAT THERE HAS BEEN A REDUCTION IN DISCRIMINATORY PRACTICES BECAUSE WHEN

EVERYONE IS IN UNIFORM, THEY LOOK ALIKE AND GET EQUAL TREATMENT. I MIGHT

ADD THAT DUE TO THE OUTSTANDING COOPERATION OF ALL PERSONNEL IN COMPLYING

WITH THE UNIFORM POLICY, A CIVILAIN CLOTHES ARE NOW PERMITTED OFF BASE

BETWEEN 0400 AND 1800 DAILY.

8. TO RETURN TO THE CHRONOLOGY OF EVENTS, ON APRIL 3RD WE MET WITH GOVERNOR

LEE, SENIOR SUPERINTENDENT YUN AND CAPTAIN CHOE TO EXPLAIN THE REASONS FOR

PLACING THE A-FRAME OFF LIMITS AND THE UNIFORM POLICY AND TO SOLICIT THEIR

COOPERATION IN MAKING CHICOL VILLE A SAFE PLACE TO VISIT.

WE ALSO MET WITH THE CLUB OWNERS LATER THAT SAME DAY. AGAIN, THEY

WERE BRIEFED ON DISCRIMINATION IN THE CLUBS AND VIOLENCE IN THE VILLE,

AND WERE REQUESTED TO COOPERATE IN SOLVING THESE PROBLEMS.

ON THE EVENING OF 19 APRIL, TWO AIRMEN WERE ASSAULTED, WITHOUT PROVOCATION,

BY FIVE UNIDENTIFIED ASSAILANTS IN THE BIG HOUSE CLUB LOCATED IN THE AREA

COMMONLY REFERRED TO AS PAPA JOE ALLEY. THIS INCIDENT LED TO SEVERAL STEPS.

FIRST, THE PAPA JOE ALLEY AREA WAS IMMEDIATELY PLACED OFF LIMITS FOR A

PERIOD OF 30 DAYS BECAUSE OF THE HIGH RISK OF HARM TO THOSE ENTERING THAT

SECTION. SECONDLY, GENERAL MCNEIL SENT TWO LETTERS TO SENIOR SUPERINTENDENT

YUN. THE FIRST, DATED 20 APRIL 1973, ANNOUNCED THE GENERAL'S DECISION TO

PLACE PAPA JOE ALLEY OFF LIMITS AND REQUESTED KNP ASSISTANCE IN PROVIDING

SUFFICIENT SECURITY PERSONNEL AND ADEQUATE LIGHTING FOR THE SAFETY OF ALL

PERSONNEL. THE SECOND LETTER, DATED 26 APRIL 1973, REITERATED THE GENERAL'S

CONCERN OVER CONDITIONS IN CHICOL VILLE AND RESTATED OUR NEED FOR INCREASED

POLICE PROTECTION, BETTER LIGHTING, AND COOPERATION FROM THE BAR OWNERS IN

AFFORDING BETTER PROTECTION FOR THE SAFETY OF ITS PATRONS AND, WHEN AN

ASSAULT OCCURS, ASSISTANCE TO INNOCENT VICTIMS.

IN RESPONSE TO GENERAL MCNEIL'S LETTERS, SENIOR SUPERINTENDENT YUN MET

WITH US ON 1 MAY. WE DISCUSSED A NUMBER OF MATTERS RELATED TO THE SAFETY

OF PERSONNEL IN CHICOL VILLE, INCLUDING THE NEED FOR ADDITIONAL, UNIFORMED

POLICE, MORE LIGHTING, AND THE COOPERATION OF BAR OWNERS AND PRIVATE

CITIZENS IN REPORTING INCIDENTS AND ACTING AS WITNESSES.

WE HAD A SIMILAR MEETING ON MAY 3RD WITH GENERAL PARK, SUPERINTENDENT

OF KYONGGI PROVINCE POLICE. AT THAT TIME WE DETAILED FOR GENERAL PARK

THE MUTUAL PROBLEMS IN CHICOL VILLE AND SOLICITED HIS COOPERATION IN

MAKING CHICOL VILLE SAFER. I MIGHT ADD THAT ON THE NIGHT BEFORE OUR

MEETING WITH GENERAL PARK, A SERIOUS INCIDENT OCCURRED IN THE ALOHO CLUB.

AN AMERICAN AIRMAN AND A ROK SOLDIER HAD A DISAGREEMENT WHICH AT FIRST

WAS BROKEN UP THEN LATER RESUMED. IT RESULTED IN THE ROK SOLDIER STABBING

THE AMERICAN AIRMAN IN THE ABDOMEN. AS A RESULT OF THIS INCIDENT, THE

ALOHA CLUB HAS BEEN CLOSED BY THE KNP AND IS OFF LIMITS FOR A PERIOD OF

SEVEN DAYS.

THAT, GENTLEMEN, BRINGS YOU UP TO DATE ON THE BACKGROUND OF THE CURRENT

SITUATION. AS GENERAL MCNEIL CHARACTERIZED IT IN HIS LETTER TO SENIOR

SUPERINTENDENT YUN, THE SITUATION IS SERIOUS. WE ARE ESPECIALLY CONCERNED

ABOUT CONDITIONS IN PAPA JOE ALLEY.

9. AS YOU KNOW, PAPA JOE ALLEY HAS BEEN A RECOGNIZED SEGREGATED AREA,

FREQUENTED ONLY BY BLACKS, WHERE 85 PER CENT OF OUR PEOPLE CANNOT GO IN

SAFETY. ITS A LONG, DARK ALLEY WITH A HONEYCOMBED NETWORK OF ENTRANCES

AND EXITS AND MULTITUDE OF SMALL MAKLI HOUSES MAKE IT EXTREMELY PERCARIOUS

FOR OUR PEOPLE. THE PAPA JOB ALLEY SITUATION IS INTOLERABLE. WE COULD,

OF COURSE, DECLARE IT OFF LIMITS FOR REASONS OF SANITATION AND KEEP IT

OFF INDEFINITELY, BUT WE FEEL THAT THIS IS NOT THE LONG TERM SOLUTION

WE NEED.

WHAT, THEN, DO WE NEED TO ATTAIN OUR MUTUAL GOAL OF MAKING CHICOL

VILLE A SAFE PLACE FOR U.S. FORCES PERSONNEL TO VISIT? I SUBMIT WE

NEED THE FOLLOWING:

10. FIRST, ADDITIONAL KOREAN NATIONAL POLICE SHOULD BE ASSIGNED TO

CHICOL VILLE, ESPECIALLY PAPA JOE ALLEY. AT PRESENT SOME 26 KNPs ARE

ASSIGNED TO THE SONGTAN-UP SUBSTATION, INCLUDING THOSE ASSIGNED TO OUR

97

OSI AND SECURITY POLICE. WE FEEL THIS NUMBER IS INADEQUATE TO COPE WITH THE

PROBLEM.

SECONDLY, WE BELIEVE THAT MORE UNIFORMED POLICE WOULD HELP REDUCE THE

PROBLEM OF VIOLENCE. THE SIGHT OF A UNIFORM ACTS AS A DETERRENT TO CRIME

AND IS RECOGNIZED AS A SYMBOL OF AUTHORITY BY OUR PERSONNEL.

THIRD, ADDITIONAL LIGHTING IS REQUIRED IN THE VILLE, PAPA JOB ALLEY

AND THE OTHER ALLEYS LEADING TO THE NIGHTCLUBS IN PARTICULAR. THEY DON'T

NECESSARILY HAVE TO BE FLOODLIGHTS. GOOD ELECTRIC LIGHTS WILL DO. AND

WHILE I'M ON THE SUBJECT OF LIGHTING, I MIGHT ADD THAT THE INTERIOR OF MANY

OF THE CLUBS IS MUCH TOO DIM FOR SAFETY.

FOURTH, THERE IS A DEFINITE REQUIREMENT FOR CLUB OWNERS AND PRIVATE

CITIZENS TO DEMONSTRATE MORE CIVIC RESPONSIBILITY. WE WOULD LIKE TO SEE A

PROGRAM DEVELOPED TO EDUCATE PEOPLE TO REPORT INCIDENTS WHEN THEY OBSERVE

THEM AND TO COME FORWARD AS WITNESSES. AT THE SAME TIME WE HAVE BEEN

EDUCATING OUR PEOPLE ALONG THE SAME LINES.

FIFTH, WE FEEL THAT LONG RANGE PLANS SHOULD BE DEVELOPED TO RELOCATE

THE CLUBS TO THE MSR. WE REALIZE THIS WILL BE COSTLY AND THAT IT CAN'T

BE ACCOMPLISHED OVERNIGHT. HOWEVER, WE BELIEVE WE SHALL ALWAYS HAVE A

PROBLEM AS LONG AS MOST OF THE CLUBS ARE LOCATED DOWN BACK ALLEYS HX AWAY

98

FROM THE MAIN STREAM. FOR THIS REASON I AM VERY CONCERNED ABOUT THE VERY

EXPENSIVE PROJECT TO CONSTRUCT THE WESTERN VILLAGE SO FAR FROM THE MSR.

FINALLY, AS HAS BEEN POINTED OUT TO THIS AD HOC SUBCOMMITTEE IN THE

PAST, WE BELIEVE THE FACT THAT CHICOL VILLE IS NOT AN INCORPORATED CITY

AND HAS NO RECOGNIZED LOCAL GOVERNING OFFICIALS SERIOUSLY HAMPERS OUR

ABILITY TO MUTUALLY SOLVE THESE PROBLEMS.

I DO NOT WISH TO LEAVE YOU WITH THE IMPRESSION THAT NOTHING IS BEING

DONE ABOUT THE PROBLEM EITHER BY US OR BY PYONGTAEK COUNTY OFFICIALS.

11. FOR OUR PART, I HAVE ALREADY MENTIONED THE UNIFORM POLICY, THE

FREQUENT MEETINGS WITH GOVERNMENT OFFICIALS AND CLUB OWNERS, AND THE

COURTESY PATROLS. IN ADDITION, AS A DETERRENT TO CRIME, WE HAVE STEPPED

UP OUR EFFORTS TO PUBLICIZE WHAT HAPPENS TO THOSE WHO BREAK THE LAW BY

PUBLISHING THE RESULTS OF COURT MARTIALS AND OTHER DISCIPLINARY ACTIONS

IN THE DEFENDER NEWSPAPER AND ON A WEEKLY RADIO PROGRAM, OSAN IN

PERSPECTIVE.

THE EFFORTS TO SOLVE THE PROBLEMS HAVE NOT BEEN ONE SIDED. WE HAVE

ENJOYED WARM, HARMONIOUS RELATIONS WITH GOVERNOR LEE, SENIOR SUPERINTENDENT

YUN AND CAPTAIN CHOE. WE KNOW THEY ARE WORKING THE PROBLEM AND THAT

UNDER THE CAMP TOWN PURIFICATION PROGRAM, THEY HAVE MADE PROGRESS IN

99

IMPROVING CHICOL VILLE BY EXPANDING AND PAVING STREETS AND ROADS AND IN

BEAUTIFYING THE CITY GENERALLY.

HOWEVER, I WOULD BE LESS THAN CANDID IF I SAID WE WERE SATISFIED WITH

ALL THAT HAS BEEN DONE. AS I MENTIONED AT THE OUTSET, OUR MUTUAL GOAL IS

TO MAKE CHICOL VILLE SAFE FOR ALL PERSONNEL --BOTH AMERICAN AND KOREAN.

WE HOPE WE ARE MOVING IN THAT DIRECTION. THANK YOU VERY MUCH.   ARE

THERE ANY QUESTIONS?

(00

기 안 용 지

분류기호 문서번호	미이 723 -	(전화번호)	전결규정 9조 2항 **국장** 전결사항
처리기간			
시행일자	1973. 5. 16.		국 장
보존년한			
보조기관	**과 장**		협 조
기안책임자	양세훈 북미2과		
경유		발	
수신	수신처 참조	신	
참조			
제목	SOFA 군민관기분과위원회 제18차 회의 대비 (의제 제4항)		

연 : 미이 723 - 16165

SOFA 군민관기분과위원회 제19차 회의에서 논의할

예정인 동분과위 제14차 보고서 초안을 별첨 송부하오니 검토

하시고 귀견이 있으시면 동회의에서 제시할수 있도록 대비하시기

바랍니다.

첨부 : 보고서초안 1부. 끝.

수신처 : 내무부장관 (지방국장, 치안국장 (외사과, 수사지도과))

법무부장관 (법무실장, 검찰국장)

교통부장관 (관광국장)

보건사회부장관 (보건국장)

문학공보부장관 (공보국장)

정와대 정무수석비서관 (내무 . 보사담당비서관)

102

내　　　무　　　부

관리 100 - 6041 (70.2481)　　　　1973.　5.　16

수신　외무부장관

참조　북미2과장

제목　SOFA 군민관계 분과위원회 회의 자료

　　1. '73 기지촌 대책사업중 중앙관계부처 사업계획이 별첨과
같사옵기 참조 바라며

　　2. 73. 5. 7 개최된 SOFA 군민관계 분과위에서 미측으로부터
건의된 사항에 대한 당부 조치결과를 별첨과 같이 보고합니다.

첨부. 1. '73 중앙관계부처 기지촌 대책 사업 1부

　　　2. 미측 건의사항 당부 조치 결과 1부　　　　끝

　　　　　　내　　　무　　　부　　　장

(03

◦ 部處別事業費總括
(單位:千元)

部處別	國費支援	地方負擔	自負擔	中央自体施行事業	合計
內務部	100,000	70,505	7,256	8,700	186,461
保健社会部	31,562	73,061		7,985	112,608
勞動庁	11,281	11,278		3,000	25,559
法務部				5,016	5,016
口防部				12,300	12,300
関税庁				41,636	41,636
中央情報部			3,833		3,833
計	142,843	154,844	11,089	78,637	387,413

註. 1. 地方費는 負担要求額임
   2. 該当 市道는 國費支援事業을 追加를 含하여
   綜合実践計劃을 樹立하여 73. 5. 25까지
   内務部로 報告하도록 措置하였음

~2~

○市道別

中央部廳의 國費支援 및 自體事業 總括

(單位 : 千원)

市道	基地村別 (市部廳別)	國費支援額			地方費			自負担	中央部廳 自體事業費		合計
		回計 (機額)	中央各部廳 部廳別	全額	計	市道費	市部費		中央各部廳 部廳別	全額	合計
서울		2.543	民.社部	2.543	50.807	50.807			部廳別	12.570.5	65.920.5
									民.社部	1.897.5	
									法務部	460.	
									治安局	1.219.	
									內務部	8.204	
									勞動부	780	
釜山		1.263	民.社部	1.263	1.951		1.951			6.198	9.412
									民.社部	615	
									法務部	240	
									治安局	903	
									內務部	4.240	
									勞動부	200	
京畿		95.829	勞動부 民.社部 內務部	95.829	76.218	35.933	40.285	5.876	部廳別	28.461.5	206.384.5
		23.910		821 2.449 15.640	10.076	192 小計 4.216	260 小計 5.100	3.500	民.社部 治安局 內務部 小計	865 967 1.618 3.450	
仁川		4.888	勞動부 民.社部	1.688 3.200	4.507	8.444 2.819 小計 3.863	8.444 小計 8.444		民.社部 法務部 內務部 小計	240 260 3.546 4.046	

普通	基地村別	国費 支拂額		地方費			個負担	中央部廠自體事業		合計	備考
		他 額	中央各部廠 部廠別 金額	計	中通費 各部費	中部費		中央部廠別 部廠別	金額		
	坡州	5.557	労動部 1.531 / 保.社部 4.026	4.479	916 3.248 / 計 3.864	615 / 計 615		保.社部 治安部 両市費 計	240 842 1.977 3.059		
	平澤	58.079	労動部 228 / 保.社部 4.800 / 内務部 52.500	54.500	240 3.846 17.305 / 計 21.391	298 / 計 33.109	2.376	保.社部 治安部 両市費 労動部 計	865 450 3.256 290 4.861		
	議政府	2.679	保.社部 2.679	1.941	1.941			保.社部 法務部 治安部 内務部 労動部 計	1.667.5 1.040 815 3.018 200 6.540.5		
	水原							法務部	1.000		
	金浦							両税局	3.373		
	漣川				350	357		治安局 計	649		
	其他	716	労動部 716	715				両税局	1.493		
										420	
計 合計								治務部 労動部	420 220 200		

市道	基地村別	國費 他部局 金額	中央各部庶 部庶別	金額	地方費 計	市道費	市郡費	自負担	中央各部庶自体事業 部庶別	金額	合計	級	方
忠南	大德	1,155		1,155	700	700				2,822	4,677		
	大田		信社部	1,155	700	700			信社部 / 治安司 / 内税庁 / 小計	365 / 207 / 2,010 / 2,582			
									法務部	240			
全北	沃溝	18,859			11,733	2,696	4,037	1,380		3,113	35,085		
	群山	16,533	労働部 / 信社部 / 内務部	1,432 / 1,741 / 13,360	8,208	816 / 1,417 / 4,200 小計 6,433	1,960 小計 2,775	1,380	信社部 / 治安司 / 内税庁 / 小計	365 / 479 / 1,989 / 2,833			
	全州	2,326	労働部	2,326	2,525	1,263	1,262		法務部	280			
慶北	大邱	23,194	労働部 / 信社部	1,149 / 1,535	13,435	6,668	6,767		信社部 / 法務部 / 治安司 / 内税庁 / 労働庁 / 小計	865 / 160 / 695 / 2,550 / 580 / 4,950	44,611		
		2,684	信社部		2,232	756 / 818 小計 1,443	224 / 65 小計 289						

費目 經費地村別	國費支辨額 他需	中央各部處 部處別	中央各部處 金額	地方費 計	地方費 市道費	地方費 市郡費	自負擔	中央各部處自體事業費 部處別	中央各部處自體事業費 金額	合計	備考
流金	20,510	勞動部 保社部 內務部	839 1,171 18,500	11,203	520 905 4,0.. 川村5,226	5,1.. 5,070 川村5,998		治安局 開發廳 勞動廳 小計	315 1,969 750 3,032		
							3,833 3,833 (中村混幣等含함)	國防部 法務部 內務廳 治安局	11,070 12,300 1,016 2,395 1,359	20,903	
其他											
總計	142,843			154,844	103,755	51,089	11,089		78,637	387,413	

108

(2) 美側 要望事項 및 措置 結果.

要望事項	措置 結果
1. 警察兵力 增員	6名을 增員措置 (30名 → 36名) • 交通 ; 17名 ~ 22名 • 勤務值 ; 5名 ~ 6名 • 專把班 : 4名 • 部隊中첨 : 4名
2. 保安燈 增設	91 燈 增設 (129燈 → 220燈)
3. 市民 協調	基地村住民 啓導 徹底
4. 뒷골목 擴張	○ 對象 ; PAPA JOE CLUB, 뒷골목 擴張 BIG HOUSE ○ 事業量 ; 延長 120메 幅 2.5ᵐ → 5ᵐ ○ 期間 ; 73.5.15 ~ 5.31 ○ 施行 ; 시마을 事業 要領 ○ 撤去 및 改補修 對象 : 建物 19 棟 告水 1 個 돌담불 3 個

※註) • 格淡邑市界拡 變경에 對하여는 現行法上 不可라므로
<del>止으─面積</del>─ 行政力 支援 强化로 가능.

109.

공   란

공   란

공   란

공 란

공 란

공   란

공   란

공   란

공   란

공　　　란

공　　　　란

공 란

공 란

공   란

공　　란

공　　란

공   란

공   란

공   란

공 란

공   란

공   란

공   란

공   란

공   란

공 란

공 란

공   란

공 란

受信 ; 外務部 ●美2課長
發信 ; 內務部 管理課長

1973. 5. 25.

邑의 市昇格에 關한 問題

○ 〈邑의 市昇格에 対하여는〉

첫째로 市는 그 大部分이 都市의 形態를
갖추어야 하는데 (地方自治法 第5條.
地方自治에 關한 臨時措置法 第3條의2)

- 都市의 形態로서는
① 市街地人口比 및 市街地面積
② 都市·産業人口比
③ 財政規模
④ 特別行政官署
⑤ 教育·文化·金融 施設
⑥ 交通·通信 施設   等
要件이 勘案 되어야 하며

둘째로 人口가 5万 이상 이어야 함.

○ 〈京畿道 楊州郡 東豆川邑과 平澤郡 松炭邑의 境遇〉

前項에 依한 都市形態로서의 諸般要件에
未達하여 現在로서는 市昇格이 어려운 失情임

○ 〈邑의 市昇格은 法律改正 事項임〉

地方自治法 第4條. 4.
地方自治에 關한 臨時措置法 第3條의2   參照

139

地方自治法

(1949年7月4日)
(法律 第32號)

改正
1949. 12. 15法33號 및 1956. 2. 13法385號
1956. 7. 法352號 1958. 12. 26法501號
1960. 11. 法563號

第1章 總則

第1節 通則

第1條 【目的】 本法은 地方의 行政을 國家의 監督下에서 地方住民의 自治로 하게 함으로써 大韓民國의 民主的 發展을 期함을 目的으로 한다.

第2條 【地方自治團體의 種類, 管轄】 (1) 本法에서 地方自治團體라 함은 大別하여 左의 2 種을 말한다.
1. 道와 서울特別市
2. 市, 邑, 面
(2) 道와 서울特別市는 政府의 直轄下에 두고라, 邑, 面은 道의 管轄區域內에 둔다.

第3條 【地方自治團體의 性格과 事務】 (1) 地方自治團體는 法人으로 한다.
(2) 地方自治團體는 그 地方의 公共事務와 法令에 依하여 그 團體에 所屬된 事務를 處理한다.

第4條 【名稱과 區域】 (1) 地方自治團體의 名稱과 區域은 從前에 依하고 이를 變更하는 以外에는 모두 法律에 依하여 이를 變更하거나 그 自治團體를 新設할 때에는 法律로써 한다.
(2) 地方自治團體를 廢置分合하거나 名稱區域을 法律로써 變更할 때에는 …

第4條의2 【地方自治團體의 所在地】
地方自治團體의 事務所所在地 …

第5條 【市로 될 수 있는 要件】
(1) 市로 될 수 있는 것은 그 大部分이 都市의 形態를 갖추고 人口 5萬以上, 邑은 2萬以上이어야 한다.
(2) 邑, 面을 廢止하거나 新設함으로써 …

第6條 【地方自治團體의 住民, 權利義務】 (1) 地方自治團體의 區域內에 住所가 있는 者는 그 地方自治團體의 住民으로 한다.
(2) 住民은 法令이 定하는 바에 依하여 …

第2節 條例와 規則

第7條 【條例】 地方自治團體는 法令의 範圍內에서 …

第8條 【罰則】 地方自治團體의 條例는 法令의 範圍 …

第8條의2 【條例와 規則의 立法限界】 市, 邑, 面의 條例나 規則은 …

第9條 【罰則의 委任】 道는 서울特別市는 …

第10條 【條例의 規則의 公布方式】 (1) 條例와 規則은 …

地方自治에關한臨時措置法

(1961年9月1日)
(法律第707號)

改正
1962. 3. 21法1037號 1963. 6. 18法1359號
1963. 12. 11法1512號 1973. 3. 12 法2580號

第一條 【目的】 本法은 地方自治行政을 能率化하고 그 正常化함으로써 地方自治行政의 發展을 圖謀하려함을 目的으로 한다. (1963. 12. 14 本條改正)

第二條 【地方自治團體의 種類】 (1) 地方自治團體는 大別하여 다음과 같이 二種으로 한다.
一. 道와 서울特別市 및 釜山市
二. 市와 郡
(2) 道와 서울特別市 및 釜山市는 政府의 直轄下에 두고라, 郡은 道의 管轄區域內에 둔다.

第2條의2 【地方自治團體의 組合】 …

第2條의3 【市, 邑으로의 名稱】 …

第三條의2 【市·邑으로의 名稱】 …

第四條 『邑, 面』의 市로의 昇格, 面은 …

第五條 【事務의 執行】 …

5. 제 20 차
   1973. 6. 15

14.

내   무   부

관리 100 - 6195   (70.2481)   1973.   5.   21

수신   외무부장관

참조   북미2과장

제목   기지촌 주민의 계도요령

1. 관리 100 - 6041 (73.5.17)과 관련입니다.

2. 당부에서는 기지촌 대책실천 사업의 일환으로 기지촌 주민 계도 기본지침을 별첨과 같이 작성하여 구시도에 시달하고

3. 구시도지사는 본 지침을 토대로 기지촌별 지역실정에 맞는 자체 세부실천 계획을 수립 실천토록 조치하였기 통보합니다.

4. 이 사항은 군민분과위 제20차 회의 및 합동위원회에 보고하여 주시기 바랍니다.

첨부. 기지촌 주민의 계도요령 2부   끝

               무   부   장   관

142

19173

General Guideline for Waging Public Campaign for Residents in Base Community Area

1. **Purpose:**

   a. To ameliorate environmental conditions.

   b. To have foreign nationals better understand Korea.

   c. To maintain close ties and cooperation with foreign troops.

2. **Measures:**

   a. Educational programs to enhance the spirit of Saemaul movement. (Movies and slides)

   b. Public campaign on Government policies and measures.

   c. Dissemination of Information on progress in Korea.

   d. Proprieties in speech, manner, dress etc.

   e. Prevention of racial discrimination.

   f. Eradication of larceny, especially those involving foreigners' properties.

   g. Improvement of environment for pleasant surroundings.

   h. Cooperation among local authorities.

143

基地村住民의 啓導要領

內 務 部

144

基地村住民의 啓導要領

1. 目的

○ 環境淳化를 爲한 住民啓導 ————┐
○ 外國人의 올바른 새 韓國觀認識 ——┘

    ┌ ○ 基地村周辺生活環境明朗化
    └ ○ 韓·美兩國間의 紐帶增進

2. 方針

○ 基地村 새마을精神의 鼓吹

○ 國威宣揚, 國民品位維持를 위한 教養実施

○ 人種差別(黑白分科)意識排除

○ 盜犯 雜犯団束徹底

○ 基地村地域住民의 精神淳化

○ 地域行政官署間의 緊密한 協調

145

3. 計 劃

　○　對象地區 : 全基地村

　○　對 象 者 :

　　　基地村 및 周辺地域住民

　　　観光休養業所業主

　　　美軍相対接客業所従事者

　　　美軍部隊従事員

　　　淪落女性

　○　啓導内容

　　가. 새마을精神教育 (映画 및 스라이드)

　　나. 政府施策의 P. R

　　다. 韓國의 発展相紹介

　　라. 言語, 行動, 服装등 올바른 礼節

~2~

166

마. 人種差別禁止 ~ 黑白紛糾未然防止

바. 对外国人関係滯犯의 根絶

사. 基地村 周辺 生活環境의 明朗化

아. 地域行政官署間의 紐帶强化

-3-

147

4. 細部実践要領

啓導内容	對象	期間	啓導要領	主管
1. 새마을 精神教育	·全主民 ·觀光業主 ·接客業従事者 ·部隊従事員 ·遊落女性	月1回	1. 새마을映画上映 2. 〃 스라이드紹介 3. 새마을 成功事例 紹介 4. 새마을책자配布 5. 優秀새마을見学 6. 基地村새마을事例 研究実践	·道 새마을課 ·道文化公報室 ·郡文化公報室 ·邑面長
2. 政府施 策의 P.R 韓國의発展 相紹介	〃	〃	1. 政府施策에 関한 映画 및 스라이드 2. 韓國의 発展相 紹介映画 및 스라 이드 3. 道政紹介스라이드	·道文化公報室 ·郡 〃 ·邑面長

148

啓導內容	対象	期間	啓導要領	主管
			4. 政府施業說明冊子 配布	
3. 言語 行動、服 裝의 을 바른 礼 節	·全住民 ·觀光業主 ·接客業從事者 ·部隊從事員 ·淪落女性	隨時	※ 班常会、自治会를 通하 教養実施 1. 対外國人 応待 基本会話指導 2. 粗雜하 母國語 또는 外國語使用 禁止 3. 外國人에 対한 親切한 面談要領 4. 外國人에 対한 亂暴한 行動禁止 5. 不親外國人에 対 한	·道企劃管理室 ·道文化公教室 ·道社会課 ·郡内務課 ·邑面長 ·郡保健所 ※ 指導責任公 務員의 指定

149

啓導內容	対象	期間	啓導要領	主管
			하 理解 및 善導 方法 6. 地域住民의 外國 軍服裝着用禁止 7. 美風良俗에 沮害되는 紊雜한 衣服 着用禁止 8. 接客業所勤務者의 統一된 服裝着用勸獎 9. 國民儀礼에 対한 敎育 및 冊子配布	
4. 人種差別(黑白人種)意識 排除	〃	隨時	※ 班常会 또는 自治会를 通한 敎養 實施 人. 美國人間의 人種	· 道社会課 · 道企劃管理室 · 郡内務課 · 郡保健所

950.

SOFA 한.미국 합동위원회 군민관계 임시분과위원회, 제16-24차. 1973 157

啓導內容	対象	期間	啓導要須	主管
			差別(黑白紛糾)을 間接的으로 調整할 수 있는 事例받은 →모든 業所에 波及 2. 住民·業所·從事者의 黑白人差別意識乃業 3. 人種差別業体→ 登錄取消等 行政的 措置 4. 黑白區分 專用業所의 一掃 5. 人種差別意識排除 刑行物 포스타揭示	·邑面長

啓導內容	対象	期間	啓導要領	主管
5. 外國人 關係 盜 犯防止	〃	隨時	※ 防犯委員會. 自治 會를 通하 教養 実施 1. 麻藥. 習慣性医藥 品의 製造. 使用 및 暗去來의 徹底 団束 2. 外換不法去來 및 不法所持団束 3. 竊盜品. 出處不明 의 은익 또는 賣 買行爲의 단束 4. 住民의 自律的申 告体制의 確立 發見者 即時申告 →管轄支署	· 道保健課 · 郡保健所 · 管轄警察署支 派出所 · 邑面長

~8~

152

啓蒙內容	對 象	期間	啓 蒙 要 領	主 管
6. 基地村 周辺生活 環境의 明朗化	·全地域住民 ·全地方行政 官署	隨時	1. 不良業所, 基準未 達業所의 是正 및 改善 2. 모든 마을周辺, 業所의 청결維持 3. 粗雜한 不法突出 場, 不良간판의 除去 4. 住民、賃客女性의 副業場活用의 擴大 5. 住民使宜施設의 運営管理	·郡內務課 ·郡게 마을課 ·郡保健所 ·管轄警察署支 派出所 ·地區邑面長
7. 地域行 政官署의 紐帯強化	·地區內모 든 行政 官署	月/回 또는 隨時	※ 基地村對策에 関 하 地區長協議会 府推	·市長、郡守 ·署長支派出所長 ·保健所長

~9~

153

啓導內容	對 象	期間	啓 導 要 領	主 管
			1. 指導. 啓蒙. 困末 等 全般的 問題點 解決에 因한 討議	· 邑面長 · 住民代表
			2. 地區內 發生事件 의 解決策講究	
			3. 外國人建議事項의 有關機關協調	
			4. 啓導實績의 報告 및 分析	
			5. 指導方案施行要領 의 統一	

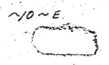

~10~E

154

기 안 용 지

분류기호 문서번호	미이 723 -	(전화번호)	전결규정 **9**조 **2**항
			국장 전결사항
처리기간			
시행일자	1973. 6. 12.		
보존년한			국 장

보조기관	과 장		협	
기안책임자	양세훈	북미 2과	조	
경유			통	
수신	수신처 참조	20886		1973.6.12
참조		발송 no. 1973 6 2	제	
제목	SOFA 군민관계 분과위원회 제20차 회의 개최			

SOFA 군민관계 임시분과위원회 제 20차 회의가 별첨과 같이

73. 6. 15. 15:30 미 8군 SOFA 회의실에서 개최됨을 알려

드리오니 이에 대비하시고 각 위원들은 필히 참석하여 주시기

바랍니다.

첨부 : 의제 1부. 끝.

수신처 :   내무부장관 (근민과장, 외사과장, 수사지도 과장)

　　　　　법무부장관 (송무과장, 검찰과장)

　　　　　보건사회부장관 (만성병담당관, 마약과장)

　　　　　교통부장관 (관광국 진흥과장)

　　　　　문화공보부장관 (해외공보관 외보과장)

　　　　　청와대 정무수석비서관 (내무.보 사담당비서관)

정서

관인

발송

AGENDA OF TWENTIETH MEETING
AD HOC SUBCOMMITTEE ON CIVIL-MILITARY RELATIONS
1530 HOURS, 15 JUNE 1973, US SOFA CONFERENCE ROOM

I.   Introduction of New Member - ROK Presentation. ✓

II.   Report on Korean-American Friendship Councils - ROK Presentation.

III. Status Reports on the Implementation of Subcommittee Recommendations - ROK and US Presentations.

IV.   Consideration of the Fifteenth Report of the Ad Hoc Subcommittee to the Joint Committee - ROK and US Presentations.
Consideration of the situation in Tonduchon - ROK and US presentations

VI.   Proposed Time for the Twenty-first Ad Hoc Subcommittee Meeting, 1530 Hours, Friday, 20 July 1973, ROK Capitol Building.

VII. Farewell to US Subcommittee Member - US Presentation. ~~(Coggans)~~

VIII. Adjourn.

156

지연증 수사지도라

美軍人 麻藥 事犯 發生 檢擧 &15

1. 檢擧 日時 場所 73. 6. 12. 15:30 頃
京畿道 坡州郡 臨津面 雲川里 崔대선 家

2. 被 疑 者 美2師團 32聯隊 1大隊
上兵 ███████████

3. 槪 要 被疑者는 73. 5月 中旬頃 泰國
방콕에 休暇次 갔다가 歸隊時
生阿片 2,303g을 航空便으로 密輸
入 (郵便) 其中 1,000g를 美國 自己집
으로 郵送하고 나머지 1,303g (16万원 相當)
를 隱匿 保管 함 20,016,000 ─
3,816,000 =

4. 檢擧 經緯 情報入手 美 CID와 合同 檢擧

5. 措 置 被疑者는 麻藥 中毒者이므로 美8軍
1452 第122 病院 入院, 繼續 搜査 中
(57)

（correction appended）

16일부터 基地村 麻藥 일제團束

告發하면 25% 補償키로

서울시는 8일 오는 16일부터 12월말까지 기지촌 일대를 대상으로 마약 및 습관성의약품 일제단속을펴기로했다.

서울시의 이같은 방침은 요즘 시내 일부 기지촌 번에 마약과 습관성의약품이 다시 나돌고 일부 유흥업소에서 「해피·스모크」가 밀매되고 있다는 정보에 따라 정해진것이다.

서울시는 이에앞서 오는 15일까지는 시내 전개업의 사회와 약사회원들을 상대로 마약 및 습관성의약품 관리상의 문제를 지도계몽 키로 했다.

중점적인 단속대상지역은 龍山區의 漢南洞·三角地·漢江路 및 永登浦區의 楊坪洞 기지촌일대와 忠武路·新村동지의 유흥업소등 이다.

시당국은 이번 단속기간 에 마약사법을 고발하는 시 민에겐 당해사건으로 부과 된 벌금·불수품 또는 추 징금의 25%를 보상금으로 지급키로 하고 일반의 협 조를 바라고 있다.

'73.6.8. <동양>

158

Narcotic & Habit forming Drug offences of

US Campside

Year	Total (Case) (Person)	Seoul	Pusan	Kyong Ki Province sub-total	Inchon	Uijong Bu	Yang Ju	Pyong Taek	Paju	Chung Nam province	Chun Buk province	Kyong Buk province	Kang Won province
72	364 (66)	57 (10)	30 (1)	176 (37)	39 (1)	35 (12)	45 (13)	51 (8)	14 (3)	38	15 (1)	48 (17)	
	469 (75)	72 (13)	38 (1)	210 (41)	47 (1)	38 (12)	51 (16)	56 (9)	18 (3)	48	23 (3)	78 (17)	
73. 3	38 (14)	1	4	22 (10)	3	8 (4)		11 (6)			2	7 (4)	2
	46 (14)	1	4	27 (10)	3	11 (4)		13 (6)			4	8 (4)	2

District Area

:: ( ) Apprehended U.S military personnel

159

Narcotics & Habit forming Drugs of US campside

Year	Heroin (g)	Codeine (Tablet)	Cocaine (Capsule)	Demerol (cc)	Morphine (Hydrochloride) (Ampoule)	Paragoric (opium tincture) (cc)	Marihuana (g)	Marihuana (Cigarettes) (ea)	Doriden (Glutethimide) (Tablets)
1971		2,040		200			24,147	2,349	57
1972	98	457	10		7	60	62,000	504	
1973. 3							9,522	174	

Year	Miltown (meprobamate) (Tablets)	Ritalin (methylphenidate) (Tablets)	Amytal (Amobarbital) (capsule)	Librax (Chlordiazepoxide) (capsule)	Tincaps (Amobarbital) (D-Amphetamine) (capsule)	Dexamyl (D-Amphetamine) (Amobarbital) (capsule)	L. S. D. (Tablets)
1971	43	19	76	110	17	25	1,978
1972							1,565
1973-3							65

Year	Mescaline (capsule)	Speed (capsule)	Librium (Chlordiazepoxide) (capsule)	Down (capsule)	Darvon (capsule)	Seconal (capsule)	Tree (capsule)	Deltazepam (capsule)
1971	347	259						
1972	483	1,047	1,683	56	159	750	2	80
1973. 3	6	5,366	28	2,243	211	3,738		

(6)

공   란

공   란

공 란

공   란

공   란

P E T I T I O N

Commanding General
Eighth United States Army
APO San Francisco 96301

16 March 1973

Dear Sir:

I extend my heart-felt appreciation and respect to you and your men for sincere and strenuous efforts to secure world peace.

We, members of this Association, have managed tourist recreation business for USFK personnel in the villages near the U.S. military camps and have provided by best service the good rest ficilities and moderate-priced liquor of every kind.

Regrettably, the military units in Dongduchon recently have taken injudicious actions as depicted in the following:

1. Korean fallen women are attracted to the clubs within the military camps. For the reason of inviting the ladies, over 200 fallen women are taken by bus or on foot every day to the clubs within the camps. Military camps, which are out of control of the Korean epidemic prevention authorities, are the places of refugees from medical inspection, hot-beds of venereal disease and also are providing the safe route to the narcotic dealers. The USFK authorities concerned, however, are ascribing the responsibilities for VD infection to us and are taking the unjustifiable measures.

2. Excessive interference in our Tourist Recreation Services.

   a. The authorities concerned frequently makes a secret inspection of our facilities and takes unilateral actions to restrict the enterance to our clubs without taking our explanation into consideration.

   b. Military Police or Security Police rushes to our clubs to check the passes and ID cards of the employees and also to search the counter desks and music rooms in our clubs. These are, we think, injudicious actions to violate the human right.

The above actions, we think, go against the Joint ROK-US campaign for purifying the villages near the military camps. For this reason, we present the petition for correcting the injudicious actions, hoping that the correcting measures should be taken as soon as possible.

Sincerely yours,

LEE, CHOON SUNG
President, The Korea Tourist
Recreation Service Association

168

미 8 군 사령관 귀하

인류의 평화를 위하여 주야 분투하시는 귀하와 뒤하 장병들의 노고에 대하여 깊은 감사와 경의를 표하는 바입니다.

당협회 산하 회원은 미군기지촌에서 주한유엔군 전용의 관광휴양업을 경영하고 있으며 유엔군의 휴양에 손색이 없는 시설과 각종주류를 염가로 제공하여 최대의 써ー미스로서 봉사하고 있읍니다. 그런데 요즘 동두천 지역부대에서 다음과 같은 부당한 처사를 하고 있읍니다. 이는 한미합동으로 추진하고 있는 기지촌 정화 사업에 역행되는 처사임으고 이의 시정을 건의하오니 빠른 시일내에 시정조치하여 주시옵기 간절히 바라나이다.

다   음

1. 한국인 윤락여성을 영내크라부에 대기 유치하고 있읍니다. 숙녀로 초청한다는 이유로 매일저녁 윤락여성 200여명을 뻐스 또는 도보로 영내크라부에 유치하고 있읍니다. 영내에는 방역당국의 단속이 미치지 못함으로 검진 미필자의 도피처가 되며 따라서 성병 전염자가 많이 발생하게 될것이며 또한 해피스모크등 마약 판매의 안전 루ー드가 되고 있읍니다.
   그림에도 성병에 걸리면 그 책임을 우리 휴양업자에게 전과시켜 출입금지등 부당한 조치를 취하고 있읍니다.

2. 관광휴양업 소에 대하여 지나친 간섭
   가. 관광휴양업소에 대하여 수시로 암행검열을 하고 있으며 한국기관이나 우리업자의 허명도 둔지 않고 일반적으로 미군출입금지 조치를 취하고 있읍니다.
   나. MP.CP.들이 업소에 들어와 종업원의 패스 명찰등을 조사하고 카운타 뮤ー직 박스를 샅샅이 뒤지고 있읍니다. 이는 인권을 유린하는 부당한 처사입니다. 끝.

서울시 중구 을지로4가 310번지   1973 . 3 . 16
삼풍 벨딍 816호실

한 국 관 광 휴 양 업 협 회

회 장 이 춘

169

공   란

공 란

공 란

공　　　란

공   란

Report on Situation in Tongduchon

1. The Korean Tourist Recreation Service Association
    and its Yangjugun District Office have submitted
    to the Ministry of Transportation a petition in
    which the Ministry is requested to take necessary
    measures to correct injudicious actions taken by
    the US military authorities in Tongduchon area.

2. The actions the Association describes injudicious
    are as follows:

    a. Over 200 business girls are taken by bus or
        on foot every evening to the clubs in the camps.
        This provides a safe route to drug traffickers
        and a good shelter to unregistered business
        girls.

    b. Unannounced inspections by US military authori-
        ties are conducted to the Korean recreation
        service establishments and off-limits are placed
        for US military personnel by unilateral actions
        taken by US authorities. Passess and ID cards
        of employees are checked and service counters,
        music boxes and other facilities in these
        establishments are searched by US MPs and CPs.

175

c. The US authorities issues to Korean stores a
   plate for US patronage which is regarded as
   an actual license for business despite the
   authorization given by the Korean Government
   authorities.

3. Based upon the petition, the authorities concerned
   conducted an investigation for fact-finding and
   the findings are as follows:

   a. It is noted that business girls are gathered
      in group on the roads adjacent to the US
      military compound, and taken into the compound
      by a USFK vehicle. The transportation to
      and from the compound is in service three
      times from 1700 to 1800 hours. Exact number
      of girls taken into the compound a day cannot
      be verified. According to the statements
      made by residents in that area, the estimate
      of number of girls are more than 200 a day.
      (Photos are attached.)

   b. The Association has provided us with a letter
      of the US military authorities dated 18 January
      1973 as an evidence that all clubs in Tongduchon

/ 176

are under a system of daily unannounced
inspections by US commanders, EOT, G-5,
Provost Marshal, CID, Preventative Medicine
and Inspector General representatives.

c. It is found that the plate for US patronage
is hung at the entrances of Korean stores
in Tongduchon area. The plate reads: "This
establishment meets acceptable standards for
US patronage." (Photos are attached.)

4. What I recommend here to this Ad Hoc Subcommittee
is to consider these situations and draw a certain
conclusion in the spirit of mutual cooperation
and friendship.

a. Inviting ladies to the compound is entirely
the independent business of US military
authorities. However, bringing business girls
into the camps every day in such a large scale
indicates a different nature from inviting
ladies for social occasions.

177

This kind of action, it is feared, might
hamper the joint ROK-US efforts to deal
effectively with the chronic problems existing
in base areas, namely, drug abuse, VD control
and black-market and larceny and, worse yet,
might eventually result in destroying the
very purpose of this Subcommittee; that is
to improve civil-military relations in camp
village areas. It is also said that such
actions by the US base authorities might
adversely affect the business activities in
the community and the existing cooperation
between the US base and the Korean community
in that area. Since the inception of this
Subcommittee the ROK Government with US
cooperation made maximum efforts to improve
the environmental conditions of the base
areas, particularly that of sanitary and
health conditions of the recreationary
establishments for the US personnel. In
many cases such efforts paid off because
local community leaders were more than
willing to cooperate with the Government

(178

authorities for better facilities and services.
Such being the case, if local communities are
to be deprived of their business in its entirety
they will have little incentive to cooperate
with the authorities for better conditions.
Admittedly, the US rights to escort in ladies
for social occasions and recreations for its
troops are not questioned. But for the best
interest of ROK-US joint efforts it is suggested
that both sides excercise moderate approaches
to this problem and refrain from daily busing
a large number of business girls into the
military compound.

179

b. It is needless to say that there is only good
   intension on the part of the US authorities
   in conducting unannounced inspections on
   Korean business establishments and placing
   the said plates. It is also known that such
   practices are being accepted in part by the
   authorities of the local community and by
   individual business owners. Nevertheless,
   there is no denying that such actions by the
   US authorities are causing considerable ill-
   feelings on the part of majority of local
   community. Particularly, placing of plates
   mentioned in effect constitute double licencing
   of business; one by Korean authority and the
   other by US authority. As for the unannounced
   inspection, the US authorities should entrust
   those aspects of inspections to proper Korean
   authorities and when the conditions are found
   to be unfit to US personnel US authorities
   should take it up with the Korean authorities
   for necessary remedial actions. In my view,
   these problems should have been handled at
   the local level and need not have been brought
   up at this Subcommittee in the first place.

(80

In any event, the problems were brought to our attention and putting aside legal aspects of the problems in question we should in all sincerity find ways to resolve these problems based on the spirit of mutual cooperation which is the back-bone of this Subcommittee.

181

Report on Situation in Tongduchon

1. Petition by KTRS Association

   a. Bringing business girls into compound.

   b. Inspections of clubs by US authorities.

   c. The plate for US patronage

2. Findings of ROK authorities

3. Recommendations

182

동두천 지역 군민 관계

1. **73. 5. 3. 한국 관광 유양업 협회 진정 (별첨 1)**

   한국 관광 유양업협회 및 동 협회 양주지부의 하기 미군당국의 부당성
   시정 조치 진정

   (1) 윤락여성 영내유지
   (2) 최저기준 간판 부착
   (3) 관광 유양업소에 대한 일방 암행 검열

2. **73. 5. 15. 협회에 대한 미군당국 서한내용 (별첨 2)**

   (1) 여성 영내 출입 엄격 통제
   (2) 일방 암행검열 실시 부인
   (3) 협회 양주지부장의 진정 사실 부인으로 협회 진정내용의 신빙성
        결여를 지적
   (4) SOFA 군민관계 분과위에서 적절히 처리됐는 문제임을 지적

3. **73. 5.22. SOFA 군민관계 주무부처 관계관 회의**

   (1) 참석자   : 고통부 진흥과장, 내무부 관리과장, 외무부 북미 2과장
   (2) 합의사항 : 미군당국, 협회본부 및 지부가 각기 상이한 주장을
                   하고 있어 우선 한국측 위원들의 현지 답사가 필요
                   하다고 합의

183

4. <u>73. 5. 25. 군민관계 한국측 위원 현지답사</u>

(1) 참석자 :   교통부 진흥과장 김철용

내무부 군미과장 백세현

외무부 북미 2과장 이상훈

외무부 북미 2과 서기관 양세훈

보사부 만성병 담당관실 황동석

내무부 치안국 황 경위

(2) 조사내용 :

(가) 윤락여성 영내유치

1) 관광협회 양주 지부장 이건차 및 동두천지구 윤락여성 단체 민들테익 (회원 2,359명) 총회장 김상수 는 매일 1700 - 1800 사이 2~3회씩 미군차량으로 윤락여성 (대부분 민들테익 회원)들이 영내로 들어가며, 영내 출입수 가 점차 증가하여 최근 에는 매일 약 2-300명으로 추산된다고 진술함.

2) 이들 진술에 의하면, 미군 영내 클럽측 이 윤락여성들의 주민등록증 과 검진증을 확인한후 승차시킨다 함.

3) 군민관계 한국측 위원들은 매일 2-300명이마는 숫자를 확인할 수는 없었으나 별첨 (3)과 같이 미군 차량에 의한 영내 출입을 확인함. 위원들이 목격한 차량번호 는 USFK Vehicle 7   이었으며, 차체에 CCA

184

NCOOM We give a damn 이라고 쓰여 있었음.

이밖에 다른 차량도 목격되었음.

(나) 미군당국의 최저기준 간판 부착

1) 관광 휴양업소뿐만 아니라 동두천지역 전역에 걸쳐 각종 상점에 미군간판이 부착되어 있음이 확인됨.(별첨 4)

2) 협력측은 이와같은 미측 처사가 사실상 미군상대 영업을 위한 허가권의 구실을 하고있어 영업행위에 대한 부당한 간섭이라고 주장함.

(다) 관광 휴양업소에 대한 미측의 일방 암행 검열

1) 미군당국이 73. 1. 18.부터 미측 관계관들로만 구성된 암행 검열을 실시하고 있음이 확인됨. (별첨 5)

2) 또한 73. 2. 21.자로 미군당국과 동두천읍 당국간에 관광 휴양업소의 운영기준에 대한 합의 서명이 있었음.

(별첨 6)

(마) 미군당국 서한에서 지적한 협력 양주 지부장의 진정사실 부인

협력 양주 지부장이 73. 5. 3.자로 교체되었음으로 진정 사실 자체 부인은 신, 구 지부장간의 알력 또는 미측과의 언어장애 때문인것으로 추측됨.

5. 대책

SOFA 군민관계 분과위원회에 이 문제를 정식으로 제기.

185

(ii) offenses arising out of any act or omission done in the performance of official duty.

(b) In the case of any other offense, the authorities of the Republic of Korea shall have the primary right to exercise jurisdiction.

(c) If the State having the primary right decides not to exercise jurisdiction, it shall notify the authorities of the other State as soon as practicable. The authorities of the State having the primary right shall give sympathetic consideration to a request from the authorities of the other State for a waiver of its right in cases where that other State considers such waiver to be of particular importance.

4. The foregoing provisions of this Article shall not imply any right for the military authorities of the United States to exercise jurisdiction over persons who are nationals of or ordinarily resident in the Republic of Korea, unless they are members of the United States armed forces.

5. (a) The military authorities of the United States and the authorities of the Republic of Korea shall assist each other in the arrest of members of the United States armed forces, the civilian component, or their dependents in the territory of the Republic of Korea and in handing them over to the authority which is to have custody in accordance with the following provisions.

(b) The authorities of the Republic of Korea shall notify promptly the military authorities of the United States of the arrest of any member of the United States armed forces, or civilian component, or a dependent. The military authorities of the United States shall promptly notify the authorities of the Republic of Korea of the arrest of a member of the United States armed forces, the civilian component, or a dependent in any case in which the Republic of Korea has the primary right to exercise jurisdiction.

(c) The custody of an accused member of the United States armed forces or civilian component, or of a dependent, over whom

— 198 —

186

United States armed forces shall have the right to police any facilities or areas which they use under Article II of this Agreement. The military police of such forces may take all appropriate measures to ensure the maintenance of order and security within such facilities and areas.

(b) Outside these facilities and areas, such military police shall be employed only subject to arrangements with the authorities of the Republic of Korea and in liaison with those authorities, and insofar as such employment is necessary to maintain discipline and order among the members of the United States armed forces, or ensure their security.

11. In the event of hostities to which the provisions of Article II of the Mutual Defense Treaty apply, the provisions of this Agreement pertaining to criminal jurisdiction shall be immediately suspended and the military authorities of the United States shall have the right to exercise exclusive jurisdiction over members of the United States armed forces, the civilian component, and their dependents.

12. The provisions of this Article shall not apply to any offenses committed before the entry into force of this Agreement. Such cases shall be governed by the provisions of the Agreement between the United States of Amearica and the Republic of Korea effected by an exchange of notes at Taejon on July 12, 1950.

(Ageed Minutes) ARTICLE XXII

The provisions of this Article shall not affect existing agreements, arrangements, or practices, relating to the exercise of jurisction over personnel of the United Nations forces present in the Republic of Korea other than forces of the United States.

Re Paragraph 1 (a)

It is understood that under the present state of United States law, the military authorities of the United States have no effective criminal jurisdiction in peacetime over members of the civilian component or dependents. If the scope of United States military

— 206 —

United States shall have the right upon request to have access at any time to members of the United States armed forces, the civilian component, or their dependents who are confined or detained by authorities of the Republic of Korea. During the visit of these persons at confinement facilities of the Republic of Korea, military authorities of the United States shall be authorized to provide supplementary care and provisions for such persons, such as clothing food, bedding, and medical and dental treatment.

Re Paragraph 10(a) and 10 (b)

(1) The military authorities of the United States will normally make all arrests within facilities and areas in use by the United States armed forces. This shall not preclude the authorities of the Republic of Korea from making arrests within facilities and areas in cases where the competent authorities of the United States armed forces have given consent, or in cases of pursuit of a flagrant offender who has committed a serious crime.

Where persons whose arrest is desired by the authorities of the Republic of Korea, and who are not members of the United States armed forces or civilian component or dependents, are within facilities and areas in use by the United States armed forces, the military authorities of the United States will undertake, upon request, to arrest such persons. Any person arrested by the military authorities of the United States who is not a member of the United States armed forces or civilian component or a dependent shall immediately be turned over to the authorities of the Republic of Korea.

The military authorities of the United States may arrest or detain in the vicinity of a facility or area any person in the commission or attempted commission of an offense against the security of that facility or area. Any such person who is not a member of the United States armed forces or civilian component or a dependent shall immediately be turned over to the authorities of the Republic of Korea.

188

— 224 —

2 The authorities of the Republic of Korea will normally not exercise the right of search, seizure, or inspection with respect to any person or property within facilities and areas in use by the United States armed forces or with respect to property of the United States wherever situated, except in cases where the competent military authorities of the United States consent to such search, seizure, or inspection by the authorities of the Republic of Korea of such persons or property.

Where search, seizure, or inspection with respect to persons or property within facilities and areas in use by the United States armed forces or with respect to property of the United States in the Republic of Korea is desired by the authorities of the Republic of Korea, the military authorities of the United States will undertake, upon request, to make such search, seizure, or inspection. In the event of a judgment concerning such property, except property owned or utilized by the Government of the United States or its instrumentalities, the United States will in accordance with its laws turn over such property to the authorities of the Republic of Korea for disposition in accordance with the judgment.

(Agreed Understanding) ARTICLE XXII
Agreed Minute Re Paragraph 1 (a)

The Government of the Republic of Korea agrees that, upon notification under the second sentence of the Agreed Minute Re Paragraph 1 (a), the military authorities of the United States may exercise jurisdiction over such persons in accordance with the terms of the Criminal jurisdiction Article.

Paragraph 1 (b)

The civil authorities of the Republic of Korea will retain full control over the arrest, investigation and trial of a member of the United States armed forces or civilian component or a dependent.

Agreed Minute Re Paragraph 2

It is understood that the United States authorites shall exercise utmost restraint in requesting waivers of exclusive jurisdiction as

189

CRIMINAL JURISDICTION

Agreed View No. 10

ⓐ USFK - KNP Joint Patrols
한미 합동 순찰

Pursuant to Paragraph 5(a) and 10(b) and Agreed Minute Re Paragraph
한미행협 제22조 제5(가)항 및 10(나)항, 그리고 10(가)항 및 10(나)
10(a) and 10(b), Article XXII, ROK-US Status of Forces Agreement, it is
에 대한 관한 합의 의사록에 의거하여 아래와 같이 합의한다.
agreed that:

Whenever practicable, and as a matter of mutual interest, maximum
필요할때는 언제나 상호 이익에 관한 사항으로서 주한미군과
use will be made of joint USFK-KNP patrols.
한국 경찰의 합동 순찰은 최대한으로 환용한다.
The establishment of these patrols will be in cooperation and
동 순찰대는 한미 양국의 관계기관이 상호 원조와 조정하에
coordination with the appropriate authorities of the United States
설치한다.
armed forces and the Republic of Korea. It is understood that United
미국 법집행당국은 미군
States law enforcement authorities have no authority or responsibility
구성원이 관련된것 외에는 대한민국 법규은 권한하는데 있어서 아무면
to enforce the laws of the Republic of Korea, other than as they pertain
근거나 책임이 없는 것으로 이해한다.
to United States armed forces personnel.

190
세면에 의한것 한미합동 순사오영지침
ㅈ.ㄷ. 19차 (67. 12. 21)
문인 2차처기 (91.9.22) Panel
603

10th JC - Incl 5
22 June 1967

These minutes are considered as official documents pertaining to both Governments and will not be released without mutual agreement.

Criminal Jurisdiction

Proposed Agreed View No. 9

Investigation of Incidents
Outside US Facilities and Areas
미국 시설 및 구역외에서의 사건의 조사

Pursuant to Paragraph 5(a) and 10(b) and Agreed Minute Re Paragraph
한미행협 제22조 제5(가)항 및 10(나)항과 제10(가)항 및 제10(나)항에
10(a) and 10(b), and Par 6(a), Article XXII, ROK-US Status of Forces
관한 합의 의사록과 제6(가)항에 의거하여 다음과 같이 합의한다.
Agreement, it is agreed that:

In incidents occurring outside U.S. facilities or areas wherein the
미국 시설 및 구역외에서 발생한 사건으로서 미국군인, 군속, 또는
initial information indicates that a member or members of the United States
그들의 가족이 미국의 전속적 재판 관할권에 속하는 사건에 관련됐다는
Armed Forces, civilian component, or dependents thereof, have been involved
것 제보가 있으면 즉시 가까운 미군 법무 집행기관에 통보한다.
in an incident which would fall within the exclusive jurisdiction of the
United States, the nearest United States Armed Forces law enforcement
agency will be notified immediately. United States law enforcement per-
이런 사건의 수사에 대해서는 미군
sonnel have the responsibility for the investigation of such incidents.
법무 집행원의 책임으로 한다.

Whenever an incident occurs outside U.S. facilities involving a member
경합된 재판 관할권에 속하는 사건으로 미국군인, 군속, 또는 그들의
or members of the United States Armed Forces, civilian component, or de-
가족이 관련된 사건이 미국-시설 외에서 발생하는 경우에는 언제나 한국과
pendents thereof, which would fall within the concurrent jurisdiction,
미국 법무 집행원은 사황에 따라서 어느곳에서든지 수사를 한다.
investigations by US and Korean law enforcement personnel shall be conducted wherever warranted by the circumstances. In all such cases, United
이런 모든 경우에 있어서
States law enforcement personnel will cooperate with and solicit the
미국 법무 집행원은 한국 법무 집행 당국자와 협력하여야 하며 또
assistance of the Korean law enforcement authorities.
협력을 청할수 있다.

In recognition of the right and obligation of United States law
법 회가 미국정부 재산 및 미국인 또는 개인재산에 관한 경우
enforcement agencies to conduct investigations in cases of offenses against
수사진행에 대한 미국 법무진행기관의 권리와 의무를 인정하여 대한민국
United States Government property and/or personnel, and their private
법무진행당국은 미국 법무진행당국의 수사진행에 모든 가능한 협조를 제공한다.
property, Republic of Korea law enforcement authorities will render all
possible assistance in investigations initiated by United States law
enforcement agencies.

1486

10th JC - Incl 5
22 June 1967

CRIMINAL JURISDICTION

Agreed View No. 8

Departure from Korea of Witnesses at Investigations
수사 도중 증인의 이한에 관한 건

Pursuant to Para 6(a), Art XXII and Agreed Minute thereto of the
한미협정 제22조 6(가)에 의거, 미군당국은 한미협정의 적용을
ROK-US Status of Forces Agreement, it is agreed that U.S. authorities
받는 사건에 대한 증인이 분원으로 이한하게 될 경우에는 이를 한국
will notify the local ROK investigative authorities if a U.S. witness
수사당국에 통고한다는 동의한다.
to a SOFA incident is due to depart Korea in the near future. The ROK
authorities will then notify the U.S. authorities at least two days before
한국당국은 만약 동증인에 대하여 증거보존 조치가 필요하다고 생각한
the witness' scheduled departure if they consider it necessary to pre-
경우에는 적어도 동증인의 이반예정일 2일전에 이를 미군당국에 통고한다.
serve any evidence he may possess.

Such preservation of evidence may consist of the examination of the
동 증거보존 조치는 한국 형사소송법 제184조에 의한 판사의 증인
witness before a judge in accordance with Article 184 of the ROK Criminal
심문 혹은 제185조에 의한 서류 또는 기타 문적증거에 대한 검증등과
Code or the inspection of documents or other real evidence in his posses-
검사나 사법경찰관에 의한 자료나 조사나 서류 혹은 기타 문적증거의
sion in accordance with Article 185 of the ROK Criminal Code, or the
검증등을 포함한다.
examination of the witness and inspection of documents or other real
evidence by the prosecutor or by the judicial police.

The U.S. authorities will insure the witness' attendance at such
미군당국은 동절차에 증인이 참석하도록 보장하며 한국당국은
proceedings and the ROK authorities will insure that such proceedings
증인의 이반예정일에 방해가 되지 않도록 동 절차를 진행한것은
are conducted in such a manner as not to interfere with the scheduled
보장한다.
date of departure of the witness.

동두천 기지촌 동향

Ⅰ. 요

미군 외출 사병 유치 위한 전용 홀 등 업체의 경기 위축으로 폐업 단계.

1. 면세 맥주 가격이 PX 가격보다 높고 지휘관 방침으로 외출자 점감.

2. 운영 방침의 쇄신 또는 영업 전환 등 업주의 대책 요망.

Ⅱ. 용

동두천 기지촌 지역에서는 오래전 부터 미군 외출 사병을 유치하고 외화를 획득하기 위해 미군 전용 홀을 마련하고 정부의 고려로 면세 맥주를 공급 판매 해왔으나 가격면에서 2홉들이 맥주 1병이 64원씩에 인수하여 130~150원씩 으로 판매하고 있는데 비해 미제 캔맥주의 PX 가격은 50원선으로 되어 있어 거의 외면되고 있을뿐만 아니라 비교적 주량이 많은 미군들은 도수 높은 소주를 시중에서 구입 음주 하거나

193

홀에 지참 음주 하면서 위안부들과 춤이나 추고
돌아가는 경향이 늘어나고 있으며, 특히 "에머슨"
소장이 미 2사단장으로 부임한 이후 장병 외출을
강력히 규제하고 검약 정신을 배양 하는데 주력
함으로서 전용 홀의 운영은 일익 불황을 면치
못하게 되어 동두천읍 광암리 소재 ⑨ 나이아가라
홀의 경우; 평상시 1일 매상고 4~5 만원이던
것이 최근에 와서는 평균 3,000 원선으로 줄어들어
이대로는 도저히 영업을 계속할수 없는 실정이라
하며, 홀 경영자들은 동 사태를 극복하기 위해서는
맥주 의존 경영을 지양하고 주류의 대중화와
토산물의 판매. 오락 종목의 확대 등 새로운
방향의 쇄신이 ✔ 불가피 하다고 지적하고 당국의
지도를 요망하고 있다함.

194

Ⅱ - 55 기지촌 동향

개 요

국제 결혼 및 여권 수속 취급 업소들이 위안부들의 무지를 기화로 고액의 수수료를 갈취.

1. 번역 및 대서 업무 인가로 여권 수속 까지 대행.

2. 업소당 연 100~500만원 소득 취하고도 세금 포탈하여 시정책 시급.

내 용

최근 동 기지촌 주변에서 주한 외국인 및 미군들과 국제 결혼하는 위안부들을 상대로 제반 수속 절차를 대행해 주고 있는 업소들이 위안부들의 저 학력으로 인한 무지를 기화로 부당한 수수료를 갈취하는 등 횡포를 자행하는 한편. 정식 인가도 없이 폭리를 추구 하면서 각종 법망을 교묘히 피하고 탈세까지 하고 있어 현지 주민들과 위안부들로 부터 비난을 받고 있다는바.

실례로 지난 73.5.18 평택군 송탄읍 신장리에

195

거주하고 있는 위안부 ███████████████

████ 가 국제 결혼에 따른 제반 이민 수속

절차를 원오피스 (대표 원동규) 와 리라오피스 (대표

리광수)에서 대행해 주도록 의뢰하자 동 업소에서는

실제 비용이 10,000 ~ 15,000 원 밖에 들지 않음

에도 부당하게 6만원을 요구하여 하는수 없이

지불한 사실이 있는데 기지촌내에 산재해 있는

이러한 업소는 당초 당국으로 부터 영문 번역 및

통역 업무를 담당 하도록 인가를 받았음에도 행정

관청에서 대행될 제반 사무를 대행 함으로서 연간

300 ~ 500 만원의 소득을 취하고도 이에 따른

세금을 포탈하고 있어 현지 주민들은 이와같은 반

사회적인 업소들의 처사를 비난하는 한편, 실제

인가된 업무 외에 부수 업무로 막대한 폭리를

취하고 있는 점을 들어 당국의 강력한 단속책을

요망하고 있다함。

196

Col. Coggins 퇴관에 퇴한 한국측 내장 연설문

It makes me extremly happy to join
Capt. sharp in extending our heartfelt
congratulations to Col. Coggins on his
promotion to the rank of Brig. Gen.

Col. Coggins has made outstanding
contributions to the work of the Ad Hoc
Subcommittee on Civil-Military Relations.
His dedicated service to our joint efforts
has been an important factor that wrought
significant improvement on ROK-US civil-
military relations.

On behalf of the Korean component
of the Ad Hoc Subcommittee, I would like
to express, once again, our sincere
appreciation for the close cooperation
and warm friendship accorded to us by
Col. Coggins.

We all wish him every success in his
new and more important assignment and also
in his future military career.

197

공   란

공 란

공   란

공 란

공   란

공　　　란

공   란

공 란

공   란

공   란

공 란

공   란

공   란

공　　　란

공   란

공   란

공   란

공   란

공   란

공   란

6. 제 21 차

   1973. 7. 20

218

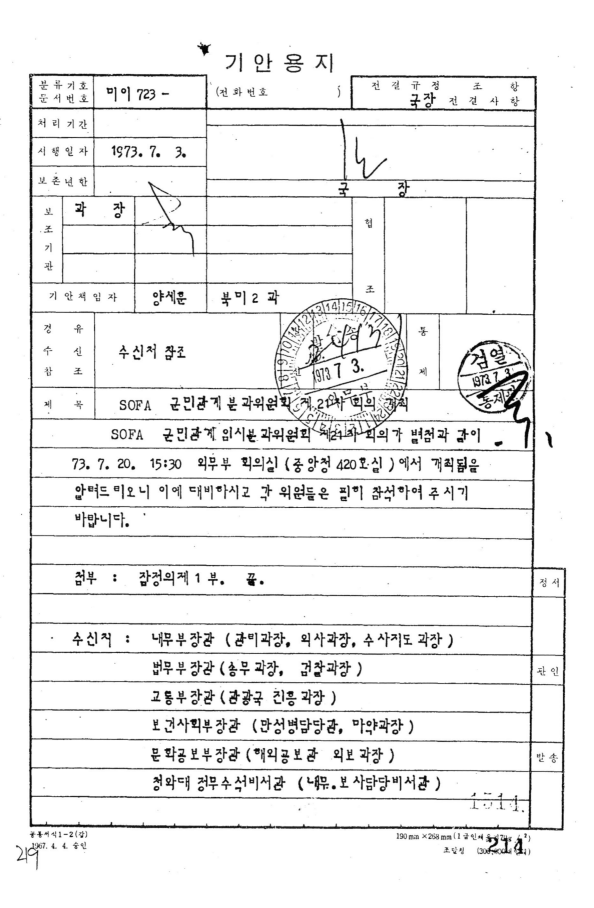

기 안 용 지

분류기호 문서번호	미이 723 -	(전 화 번 호)	전결규정 조 항 **국장** 전 결 사 항
처 리 기 간			
시 행 일 자	1973. 7. 3.		
보 존 년 한		**국 장**	
보 조 기 관	**과 장**	협	
		조	
기 안 책 임 자	양세훈 북미 2 과		
경 유		통	
수 신	수신처 참조		
참 조		제	
제 목	SOFA 군민관계 분과위원회 제 21 차 회의 개최	

SOFA 군민관계 임시분과위원회 제 21 차 회의가 별첨과 같이

73. 7. 20. 15:30 외무부 회의실 (중앙청 420호실) 에서 개최됨을

알려드리오니 이에 대비하시고 각 위원들은 필히 참석하여 주시기

바랍니다.

첨부 : 잠정의제 1 부. 끝.

수신처 : 내무부장관 (군비과장, 외사과장, 수사지도 과장)

법무부장관 (송무 과장, 검찰과장)

교통부장관 (관광국 진흥 과장)

보건사회부장관 (만성병담당관, 마약과장)

문화공보부장관 (해외공보관 외보 과장)

청와대 정무수석비서관 (내무.보 사담당비서관)

TENTATIVE

AGENDA OF TWENTY-FIRST MEETING
AD HOC SUBCOMMITTEE ON CIVIL-MILITARY RELATIONS
1530 HOURS, 20 JULY 1973, ROK CAPITOL BUILDING

I.   Welcome to New Members of Ad Hoc Subcommittee -
        ROK and US Presentations.

II.   Report on Developments Regarding Korean-American
        Friendship Councils - ROK and US Presentations.

III.   Status Reports on the Implementation of
        Subcommittee Recommendations - ROK and US
        Presentations.

IV.   Consideration of the Sixteenth Report of the
        Ad Hoc Subcommittee to the Joint Committee -
        ROK and US Presentations.

V.   Developments Relating to Isolated Base Problems -
        US and ROK Presentations.

VI.   Consideration of Situation in Tongduchon-2d US
        Army Division Area - ROK and US Presentations.

VII.   Proposed Time for the Twenty-Second Ad Hoc
        Subcommittee Meeting, 1530 Hours, Friday, 24
        August 1973, US SOFA Conference Room.

VIII.   Adjourn.

220

공   란

공   란

공　　　란

공 란

공   란

공   란

공　　　　란

공　　　란

공   란

공　　　란

공   란

공 란

공   란

공 란

공　　　란

공   란

공   란

73. 7. 20

第21次軍民關係分科委員會
報　告　事　項

內　務　部

238

目　　　　次

239

1. 韓美親善協議会 階層別 構成図 変更

　가. 韓美親善協議会 階層別 構成図中 慶尚南道 昌原面 全域이 地
　　 方行政区域 改編에 따라 '73.7.1字로 馬山市로 編入되었으
　　 므로 市郡単位協議会는 馬山市에, 基地村単位協議会는 馬山市
　　 東部出張所에 構成토록 措置하였음을 通報함.

　나. 変更措置된 慶尚南道 韓美親善協議会 構成図는 別添参照

-1-

240

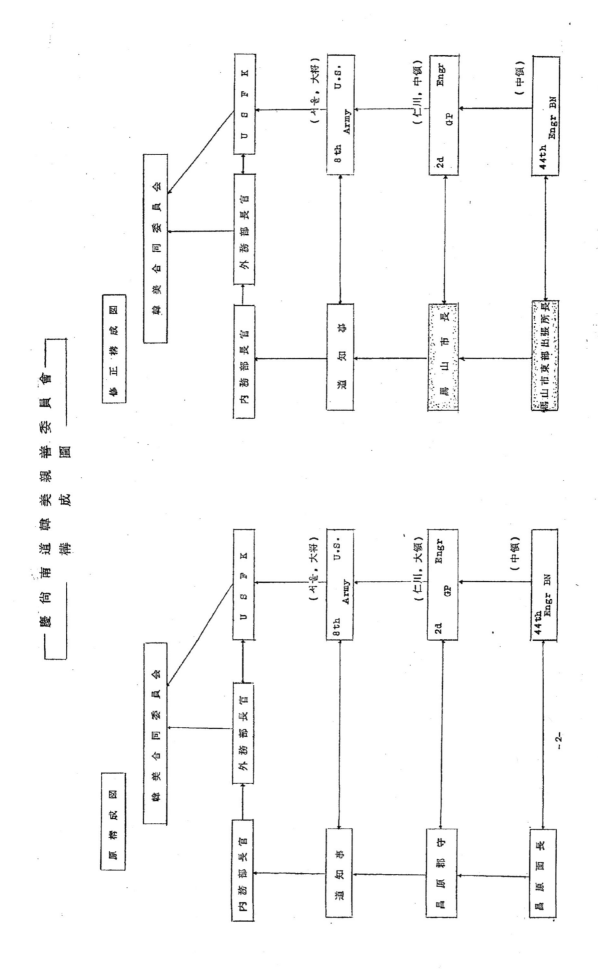

慶尙南道韓美親善委員會
稱 成 圖

修正構成圖

韓美合同委員會

外務部長官　　　　　內務部長官

UK　　　　　S　　　　　F　　　　　K

U.S.
8th Army　（서울, 大将）

Engr
2d GP　（仁川, 中領）

44th
Engr BN　（中領）

道知事

馬山市長

馬山市東部出張所長

原構成圖

韓美合同委員會

外務部長官　　　　　內務部長官

UK　　　　　S　　　　　F　　　　　K

U.S.
8th Army　（서울, 大将）

Engr
2d GP　（仁川, 大領）

44th
Engr BN　（中領）

道知事

昌原郡守

昌原面長

-2-

2. 美 8 軍 例規 550-5 号에 対한 再修正 要求

가. '73.6.15 第 20 次 軍民分科委員会에서 報告한 바와같이 韓
国側(内務部)은 地方自治団体에서 施行할 規則 準則을 市道
에 示達하고 韓美親善協議会를 7 月 10 日字로 発足完了하였음.

나. '72.6.1 美 8 軍 例規 550-5 号의 内容은 '73.6.15 軍民関
係分科委員会 第 20 次 会議時 報告된 内容(別添参照)과 많
은 部分에 있어 一致하지 아니하며, '72.1.15 例規를 検討結
果 修正된 部分은 다음 事項뿐임.

区 分	'71.1.15 例 規	'72.6.1 例 規
4. 定義	다. 地域社会와 関聯된 計劃: 司令部의 機能은………………및	다. …………………………………………및
	" 地域社会의 尊敬과 信義를 받도록 計劃을 作成한다.	" 地域社会와 司令部間의 相互尊敬과 信義 및 親善을 増進시키도록 計劃을 作成한다.
9. 構成	나. 韓国側 構成員…………………………과	나. 韓国側 構成員:………………………과
	" 地域事業家, 新聞社代表 및 労動関係 公務員이 包含된다.	地域事業代表 및 労動機関이 包含된다.

-3-

'242

区 分	'71.1.15 例 規	'72.6.1 例 規
11. 節次	카. 添 加	카. 공표 ‣ 8軍側 発表는 적정한 公報担当 혹은 공공 정보 機関을 통해서만 행해진다.

其他 o Ac of Ss Gl   P A O

   o AR 600-15   AR 210-7

   o EAGP-CM   EAPA-CR 로 修正됬음.

다. 美軍当局은 1972.6.1 美8軍 例規 550-5号를 '73.6.15

   軍民分科委員会 20次 会議時 報告된 内容中 別添 (美8軍

   例規 第550-5号에 対한 要修正 事項 調書) 과 같이 改正해

   주길 바람.

-4-

'243

第 8 軍 例 規 5 5 0 - 5 号 에 對 한 要 修正事項關書

區分	例規	意見	備考
1.目的	‥‥‥協議会의 目的은 美軍人과 韓国人間의 理解를 促進하고 改善하며 大韓国民의 社会的, 経済的 発展에 寄与하는데 있다.	‥‥‥, 協議会의 目的은 美軍人과 韓国人間의 相互間의 理解를 解를 促進하고 親善을 図謀하고 親善을 増進하고 있는데 있다.	協議会의 方向転換 ○韓国의 対한 認識 感의 刷新 ○国威宣揚
6.指針	아·(新設)	아·韓美合同委員会에서 相互合意된 事項은 両側이 誠実히 이를 遵守하고 履行할 義務를 진다. · 新協議会設立 · 을 · 協議会設立 · 으로 修正	
7.新協議会 設立	나·新協議会는 特定한 地域 軍部隊長과 計劃된 委員会로 設立으로 地域社会의 代表하는 地域軍部隊長은 地方公務員에 対하여 協議会를 設立한다. 가·任意의, 그리고 諮問的性質 및 委員会의 協議会의 設立과 運用으로 能力과 相互 限界, 이 協議会의 利益의 対하여 分明히 연이어지는 相互間의 利益의 対하여 分明히 밝혀야 한다.	나·協議会는 ‥‥‥ 된다·地域軍部隊長은 隷下将兵으로 하여금 本協議会가 韓美合同委員会의 決定으로 設立된 協議会의 目的과 機能 等을 周知케 하여야 한다.	地域部隊長의 遵守義務를 明示
8.委員会의 解散	가·部隊의 閉鎖에 関하여(軍保安이 許容하는 内) 承認을 받는 대로 地域社会代表에게 通知한다.	가·部隊의 閉鎖에 関하여 (軍保安이 許容하는 内) 承認을 받는 대로 韓国側委員会 議長에게 通知한다.	
9.構成	나·韓国側 構成員:韓国側 代表는 地域社会指導者에 依하여 決定된다.	나·韓国側 構成員은 韓国側 議長은 地方行政機関의 長(道知事·市長·郡守·区廳長 및 邑·面長)이 되고 委員은 아래 総関의 代表 또는 構成員中에	○委員長은 当然職으로 하고 構成員도 로 限定

-5-

区分	規例	意見	備考
	一般的으로 韓国側 委員은 道·特別市·郡·面·里·邑·区 或은 洞의 最高位者로서 韓国側構成員의 議長이 되며 美軍構成員이 対한 民間人 相対役이 된다. 高位公務員과 同級이고 그들과 独立된 韓国審察의 代表는 韓国側 構成員에 必須要員이 된다. 代表者는 韓設받는 部落의 高齢者, 予備軍, 健康, 衛生, 教育関係公務員과 [地域事業家, 新聞社代表 및 労動関係公務員이 包含된다.] [地域専業 代表 및 労動機関이 包含된다.] (1972.6.1)	서 議長이 指名 또는 委嘱한다. ○ 司法機関(検察, 審察, 税関) v 労動行政機関 v 保健衛生機関 ○ 情報機関 ○ 諮問委員会 또는 開発委員会 v 観光業体, 遊興業 및 料食業協会 ○ 業態婦 代表 ○ 其他 有関機関 또는 住民代表	○第70次 韓美合同委(72.1.28) SOPA 韓美合同委에서 · 適切한 水準의 代表·로 構成 토록한바 있음. [V項의 内容은 72.6.1日 例規에 있음.]
11. 節次	가. 会合: 会合은 毎月 計劃되어야 한다. 会合을 最小 60日間 開催하지 못한 때는 会合을 가질 수 있는 状況을 書面으로 提出하여야 한다.	가. 会合: 会合은 毎月 1回 定期的으로 開催하고 会合을 一方의 要請이 있을 때는 随時 開催한다. 会合을 最小 60日間 開催하지 못한 때는 会合을	随時 開催할 수 있는 融通性 敷与

區分	例規	意見	備考
	將軍이 主宰하는 委員會에서는 위의 條項이 適用 되지 아니하며 適當하다고 생각되는 때를 選定할 수 있다. 사. 小委員會의 利用 아. 未解決된 事案 : 下級委員會 水準에서 未解決된 事案은 上級司令部에 移牒한다. 協議會에서 解決되지 못한 安全問題는 陸軍省 安全官에게 提出하여야 한다.	가칫수 없는 狀況을 番面으로 提出하여야 한다. 道知事와 將軍이 主宰하는 委員會에서는 위의 條項이 適用되지 아니하며 適當하다고 생각되는 때를 選定할 수 있다. 사. 小委員會의 利用 : 削除 : 不要 아. 未解決된 事案 : ………………………………… 이 경우 他方의 곳이 上級機關이 地理的으로 遠隔한 곳에 位置하고 있을 때에는 小委員會로 하여금 相対方의 協議會와 接触하고 協議토록 하여 解決한다. 上部司令部에서도 解決되지 못한 事案은 合同委員會(軍民関係分科委員會)에 建議하여 処理토록 한다. 가. 参考人의 協議會 出席 協議會는 必要한 경우에 附議된 案件에 関聯되는 関係人 参考人의 出席要請이나 参考資料의 提示를 要請할 수 있다.	○小委員會가 解決토록 하므로써 全委員이 他 地域으로 出張가는 煩雜을 避하고자 함.(特히 行政區域이 다른 경우) ○協議事項의 圓滑, 迅速한 解決을 爲하여 追 加揷入

-7-

246

3. 忠南企劃管理室 報告事項

o 大邱所在 Korea Support Command 가 '73.6.30 解体되었
다는 報告가 있음.

確認

美8軍司 民事処에 確認한바 同 事実이 確認되었음.

問題点

忠南道 韓美親善協議会 構成을 為한 美軍側 部隊를 選定하여
야 함.

通報

美側에서 当該事実에 対하여 通報해주길 要望

※ 19支援団이 서울에서 大邱로 移動되었다 함.

-8-

247

Report to the 21st Civil-Military Sub-Committee meeting

S. H. Baek

Ministry of Home Affairs

248

CONTENTS

249

1. REARRANGEMENT OF A REGIONAL UNIT OF KOREAN-AMERICAN FRIENDSHIP COUNCIL

a. As I used to, I am glad to notify you of the fact that the district of Changwon-myon, Kyongsangnam-do was incorporated into Masan City as of July 1, 1973 according to the reorganization of administrative local units, which managed to result in the rearrangement of some reginal units of KAFC--Changwon Gun-2nd Engr Gp Council alternated as Masan City-2nd Engr Gp Council, and Changwon-myon-44th Engr Bn relations would be alternated by the Council between East Branch Office of Msan City and 44th Engr Bn.

b. Hance, the changed structure of KAFC Council between Kyongsangnam-do and U.S. Forces is digrammatized as stated in the accompanying documents.

-1-

250

2. A PROPOSAL FOR REAMENDMENT OF EUSA REG 550-5

a. Having the report on the 20th Civil-Military Sub-Committee on June 15, 1973, Korean Counterpart (Ministry of Home Affairs) gave the directions on the regulation relative to the application of Reg 550-5, and established KAFC Councils at the date of July 10.

b. The implied substances of EUSA Reg 550-5 of June 1, 1972 are much different from what was reported at the 20th meeting of Civil-Military Committee held on the fifteenth of June 1973 (as shown in the accompaning decuments). Articles as 4, 9 and 11 were amended such only in the Regulation of June 1, 1972.

Article	71, 1. 15 Reg	72. 6. 1 Reg
4. Definitions	c. --- and initiates programs to earn community respect and confidence	c. --- and initiates and sustains programs to increase command-community mutual respect, confidence, and friendship.

-3-

251

Article	71. 1. 15 Reg	72. 6. 1 Reg
9. Composition	b.----: Representatives, in addition to respect village elders, may include ---- as well as local business-men, representative of the Korean press and labor officials	b.----. Representatives, in addition to respected village elders, may include ----, as well as representative local basinesses and labor organization.
11.Procedures	k. Addition	k. publicity. ---- ----. The releases on the Eighth Army side will be made only through the apprepriate Public Affairs or Public Information Office

The others: Ac of SsG1 ⟶ P A Q

AR 600-15 ⟶ 210-7

EAGP-CM ⟶ EAPA-CR

-4-

252

c.　Therefore I would like to recommend again ~~that~~ E.A. Reg 550-5 of June 1, 1972 to be amended as what was illustrated in the accompanying document (title: Proposals for the Amendment of EA Reg 550-5) which had reported on the 20th meeting of Civil-Military Committee on June 15, 1973.

- 5-

253

Systematic Layout of Kyongsang-Nam-Do KAFC

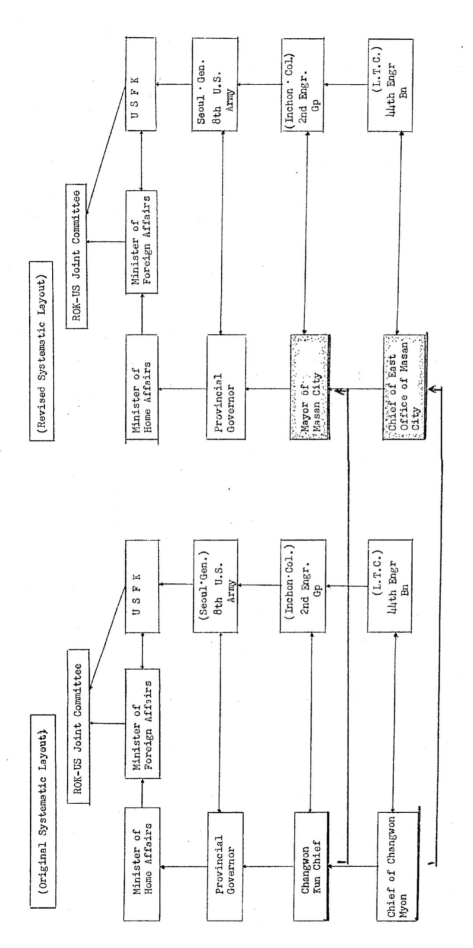

(Original Systematic Layout)

(Revised Systematic Layout)

-2-

PROPOSAL FOR REAMENDMENT OF EUSA REG 550-5

Article	EA Reg 550-5	Proposed Contents to Amand	Reference
1. Purpose	---- and contribute to the economic and sociological development of the Republic of Korea (ROK).	to rescind	Limitation of the purpose of the council
6. Policy	to add	h. Matters agreed at KAFC meetings will be sincerely observed and put into effect by each side.	
7. Establishment of new councils	b. ---- the local commander will make clear to the local official the voluntary and advisory nature of the council, its capabilities and limitations, and the mutual benefits which may be gained from its establishment and operation.	b. ---- the local commander will make clear to the officers and soldiers under his command that the council is established by mutual agreement between Eighth Army and Korean Government as well as its purpose and functions.	Identification of the local commander's duties
8. Dissolution of a council	a. Community leaders --------- camp closure.	The ROK chairman will be informed ----------- ------ camp closure.	
9. Composition	b. Korean component. Korean representation will be determined by local community leaders	b. Korean component. The head of local governments (province, city, gun, gu, uep and myon) will be the ROK chairman, who will appoint or request other representatives.	The chairman should be the head of the appropriate each local authorities. The 70th Korean-American SOFA committee (72. 1. 28)

-6-

Article	EA Reg 550-5	Proposed Contents to Amend	Reference
	----- Representatives of the --------	----- Representatives of the judicial offices (prosecutor, police, customs) are an indispensable addition to the Korean component.	described the representation as "the appropriate level of representation.
	-------- and labor officials.	Representatives may include labor, health, sanitation and information officials, as well as advisory members or developmental committee members on local area, the association of sightseeing, amusement and restaurants, the representative of service girls and the representation of concerned organizations or community leader.	Labor, health and sanitary officials and the association of sightseeing amusement and restaurants are included in the Regulation of June 1, 1972.
11. Procedures	a. Meetings. Meetings will be scheduled each month -----------------------------	Meetings will periodically be held each month and at any time when either of both components requires	The flexibility of meeting is necessary.
	-------- Those councils co-chaired by general officers are exempt from above provisions and -----------	-------- Those councils co-chaired by the provincial governor and general officers are exempt from above provisions and -----------	

-7-

Article	EA Reg 550-5	Proposed Conents to Amend	Reference
	g. Use of sub-committees	to rescind	
	h. ----- safety problems which cannot be resolved by a council willbe submitted to the appropriate Department of the Army career safety officer.	h. ----- Where the higher headquaters is far from the lower council, the safety matters will be rather be resolved through the negotiation between the panel and its higher counterpart.	h. Having the panel the solution, it could avoid to trip all members to other area. (This is necessary especially in the case of differential administrative units).
		The matters couldn't solved even at the higher headquaters would be submitted to Korean American Joint Committee (Civil-Military Council) for final resolution.	
	to add	e. Concerned persons' presence at the meeting The council will ask for the presence of persons concerned with the agenda for utterance or presentation of data, as the occasion calls for.	The attempt for the prompt resolution of agenda.

-8-

3. DISORGANIZATION OF KOREA SUPPRT COMMAND

(Contents)

The Korea-Support Command in Daegu had disbanded.

(Acording to the report from Choong Chung-Nam-Do on June 30, 1973)

(Referrence)

The informed facts was proved in accordance with the referrence to EUSA.

(Considerable Problem)

It is considerable thing to choose by the U.S. component of KAFC in Chunchung-Nam-Do.

(Notification)

The matters of concerning with this action should be notified to the Korean Authority.

* 19th Support Command is reported to have moved from Seoul to Daegu.

- 9 -

9. 제 22 차
1973. 9. 25

259

기 안 용 지

분류기호 문서번호	미이 723 -		(전화번호)	전결규정 조 항 **국장** 전 결 사 항		
처 리 기 간						
시 행 일 자	1973. 8. 20.			₩		
보 존 년 한				국 장		
보 조 기 관	과 장			협		
기 안 책 임 자	양세훈	북미 2 과		조		
경 유 수 신 참 조	수신처 참조					
제 목	SOFA 군민관계 분과위원회 제 22차 회의 개최					

SOFA 군민관계 임시분과위원회 제 22 차 회의가 별첨과 같이

73. 8. 31. 15:30 미 8 군 SOFA 회의실에서 개최됨을 알려

드리오니 이에 대비하시고 각 위원들은 필히 참석하여 주시기

바랍니다.

		경 시
첨부 : 의제 1 부. 끝		
수신처 : 내무부장관 (관리과장, 외사과장, 수사지도 과장)		관 인
법무부장관 (송무과장, 검찰과장)		
보건사회부장관 (만성병담당관, 마약과장)		
교통부장관 (관광국 진흥과장)		발 송
문화공보부장관 (해외공보관 외보 과장)		
청와대 정무수석비서관 (내무.보 사담당비서관)		

260

기 안 용 지

분류기호 문서번호	미이 723 -	(전화번호)	전 결 규 정 조 항 국장 전 결 사 항		
처 리 기 간					
시 행 일 자	1973. 9. 17.				
보 존 년 한			국 장		
보 조 기 관	과 장		협		
기 안 책 임 자	양세훈	북미 2 과			
경 유 수 신 참 조	수신처 참조		발 신	1973. 9. 20 외무부	

제 목   SOFA 군민관계 분과위원회 제 22차 회의개최

SOFA 군민관계 임시분과위원회 제 22차 회의가 별첨과 같이

73. 9. 25. 15:30 미 8 군 SOFA 회의실에서 개최됨을 알려드리오니

이에 대비하시고 각위원들은 필히 참석하여 주시기 바랍니다.

첨부 : 의제 1 부.   끝.

수신처 :   내무부장관 (관리과장, 외사과장, 수사지도 과장)

법무부장관 (송무과장, 검찰과장)

보건사회부장관 (만성병담당관 , 마약과장)

교통부장관 (관광국 진흥과장)

문화공보부장관 (해외공보관 외보 과장)

청와대 정무수석비서관 (내무.보 사담당비서관)

TENTATIVE

AGENDA OF TWENTY-SECOND MEETING
AD HOC SUBCOMMITTEE ON CIVIL-MILITARY RELATIONS
1530 HOURS, 25 SEPTEMBER 1973, US SOFA CONFERENCE ROOM

I.   Introduction of New Members of Ad Hoc Subcommittee -- ROK and US Presentations.

II.   Report on Developments Regarding Korean-American Friendship Councils - ROK and US Presentations.

III.   Status Reports on the Implementation of Subcommittee Recommendations - ROK-US Presentations.

IV.   Developments Relating to Isolated Base Problems - US and ROK Presentations.

V.   Discussion of Hospitalization of Korean Patients - US and ROK Presentations.

VI.   Proposed Time for Twenty-Third Ad Hoc Subcommittee Meeting, 1530 Hours, Friday, 26 October 1973, ~~ROK Capitol Building.~~ US SOFA Conference Room

VII.   Adjourn.

262

공   란

공　　　란

공   란

공   란

공   란

공 란

공 란

공 란

第22次軍民分科委員會報告事項

內 務 部

271

第22次 軍民分科委員會 報告事項

報 告 事 項

- o 条例公布状況

- o 協議会 委員 確定

- o 美軍側 協調要望

一. 條例公布

- o KAFC 設置의 法的 根拠인 条例를 '73·6·15 20次 軍民分科
  委員会 会議時 提出한 韓美親善協議会 設置条例 準則에 依拠
  制定 公布

  公 布 : 68個 協議会

  但 : 京畿道·水原市·安養市·富川郡·仁川市 北区·坡州郡
    衙洞面은 美軍部隊 移動등으로 条例制定 不要

二. 韓美親善協議會 委員 確定

- o 韓美親善協議会 (総 68個 協議会)의 韓国側 委員이 確定되었
  음.

  但, 京畿道 水原市·安養市·富川市·仁川市 北区·坡州郡 衙洞
  面은 美軍部隊 移動으로 委員会 構成 不要

272

三. 美軍側 協調

o KAFC 韓国側 委員이 確定되었으니 美軍側에서도 傘下 部隊에 下命하여 KFAC 美軍側 委員을 조속히 確定해 주기 바람.

o 38 대 공포 여단, 314 비행사단 (경기도에 있음) 에서 参謀진 이 없다고 協議会 構成에 非協調的이니 美軍側은 傘下 部隊 長으로 KAFC 委員으로 삼아 協議会를 構成하도록 協調바람.

273

결 번

넘버링 오류

Report to the 22nd AD HOC Sub-Committee meeting

Ministry of Home Affairs

L. H. Baek

275

Report to the 22nd AD HOC Sub-Committee
Meeting

< Contents of Report >

o Proclamation of Regulations

o Nomination of Council Members

o Close Cooperation with American Army

1. Proclamation of Regulations

The regulations - the legal basis of the Korean American

Friendship Council, were made on the basis of Working Rule

for Regulations Concerning the Establishment of KAFC which

was made public at the 20th AD HOC-Sub-Committee Meeting held

on June 15, 1973.

Those were proclamed by 68 councils, but 5 councils (Suwon

City, Anyang City, North District of Inchon City, Puchon

County, Adong Meon of Paju County) don't have to be composed

due to the movement of American Army Troops, etc.

2. Nomination of Korean American Friendship
   Council Members

The Korean components of the Korean American Friendship

2176

council, were nominated ~~included~~ except 5 council; Suwon
City, Anyang City, North District of Inchon City, Puchon County,
Adong Meon of Paju County.

3. Close Cooperation with American Army

Though the Korean members were nominated, the American members
in most of the councils were not.

We want you direct the chieves of American Army troops and
nominate your council members as fast as you can.

Especially, we stress the need of close cooperation with
"38th Arty Brigade" and "314 Air Division" located at Kyonggi
Province whose nomination of the council members is reserved,
according to the report of Kyonggi Province, because of short
of the staffs enough to compose the council.

277

8. 제 23 차

　　1973. 10. 30.

278

기 안 용 지

분류기호 문서번호	미이 723-	(전화번호)	전결규정 조 항 국장 전결사항
처리기간			
시행일자	73. 10. 18.		국 장
보존년한			
보조기관	과 장		협조
기안책임자	양세훈	북미 2과	
경유 수신 참조	수신처 참조	발송 1973 10 19 No. 29953 외무부	통제 검열 1973.10.19 통제관
제 목	SOFA 군민관계 분과위원회 제 23차 회의 개최		

SOFA 군민관계 임시 분과위원회 제 23차 회의가 별첨과 같이 73. 10. 26. 15 : 30 중앙청 외무부 회의실 (420호) 에서 개최됨을 알려 드리오니 이에 대비하시고 각 위원들은 필히 참석하여 주시기 바랍니다.

첨부 : 의제 1부. 끝.

수신처 : 내무부 장관 (관리과장, 외사과장, 수사지도과장)
법무부 장관 (송무과장, 검찰과장)
보건사회부 장관 (만성병담당관, 마약과장)
교통부 장관 (관광국 진흥과장)
문화공보부 장관 (해외 공보관 외보과장)
청와대 정무수석 비서관 (내무. 보사담당 비서관)
국방부 장관 (인사정책 담당관)

정서 / 관인 / 발송

공통서식 1-2 (갑)
1967. 4. 4 승 인

190mm×268mm 중질지 70g/㎡
조 달 청 1000 000매 인쇄)

279

TENTATIVE
AGENDA OF TWENTY-THIRD MEETING
AD HOC SUBCOMMITTEE ON CIVIL-MILITARY RELATIONS
1530 HOURS, 26 OCTOBER 1973, ROK CAPITOL BUILDING

I.   Introduction of New Members of Ad Hoc Subcommittee-
        ROK Presentation.

II.   Status Reports on the Implementation of Subcommittee
        Recommendation-ROK-US Presentations.

III.   Consideration of Situation in Songtan-eup-US Osan
        Air Base-US and ROK Presentations.

IV.   Discussion of Hospitalization of Korean Patients-
        US and ROK Presentations.

V.   Proposed Time for Twenty-Fourth Ad Hoc Subcommittee
        Meeting, 15 30 Hours, Friday, 23 November 1973, US
        SOFA Conference Room.

VI.   Adjourn.

280

미군 관련 한국인 병상자 입원문제

회의 참석자 명단 :   73. 10. 23.
                      복미2과

소 속	직 위	성 명
외무부 송무과	건관 주사 (박화태 검사 대리) →2802	이 원재
보사부 의정과	보건도 조성 요원	전종권

`281

미군 관련 한국인 병상자의 입원 문제

1. 미측이 내세우는 문제점 :

   가. 미군 병원 치료 현황 :
      (1) 미군 주둔으로 인한 한국인 병상자 치료
      (2) 치료 내용 : 응급 또는 단기 치료

   나. 문제점 :
      (1) 장기 (30일 이상) 치료의 경우 : 의사, 병원장 및
          미군의 감의동의 필요
      (2) 치료비 문제로 인한 한국 병원의 입원 기피
      (3) SOFA 청구 절차의 복잡성 및 지연
      (4) 본인에 대한 보상금의 직접 지불
      (5) 한국 병원 입원 수속시의 입원보증금 애로

   다. 제의 내용 :
      한미 심무 소위원회 구성 및 문제점 검토
      (1) 보상 책임자의 신속한 결정
      (2) 한국 병원 당국에 대한 지불 보증 방법
      (3) 한국 전 지역에 적용할수 있는 통일된 절차 강구

2. 아측의 당면 과제 :

   가. 문제점 검토 :
      (1) 보상 문제
      (2) 입원 문제

282

나. 기구 설치 문제 :
    (1)   한미 실무 소위원회 구성
    (2)   SOFA 해당 분과위원회

⊕ SOFA 감정권 부여 : 각체목여
         단계적 참여

283

공　　　　란

공   란

공   란

공 란

공　　　란

공   란

공   란

공　　　　란

공　　　란

공   란

공　　　란

공　　　란

공   란

공 란

공　　　　　란

공   란

Report to the 23rd AD HOC
Sub-Committee meeting

M O H A

S. H. Baek

300

SUBJECT: IMPROVING ENVIRONMENT AROUND THE AMERICAN
MILITARY BASES IN PYONGTAECK COUNTY

1. The MOHA has been, in order to encourage the people to
   participate in the new village movement as well as to make
   such a community in which US soldiers enjoy and live at
   ease, working on a number of projects improving environments
   around the US Army Units.

   As part of endeavours, the MOHA has selected Songtan-Eup
   in Pyongtaeck County and spent ₩ 105,000,000 for the
   following projects during the past 6 months.

2. What we had done during the past 6 months are :

   * Completed projects

       o Widening and paving the roades covering an area of
         190a

       o Paving the pedestrian streets covering an area of 93a

       o Building the roades covering 681 m

       o Moving for installment 12 electric poles.

       o Building 1,391m of sewage system

       o Building 100m of the sewage covers

       o Installing 185 street lights

       o Improving 222 poor houses

       o Eliminating 41 poor houses

301

o Purchasing a night-soil disposal car

* Besides these projects, the MOHA has been working on
making greens around the compound, installing guard
rails, paving the alleys, etc.

3. Particulary, the MOHA has completed the two water work
projects with W 50,870,000 so that the people can access
to clean water.

4. In addition, I'll make a remark on the operation of the
KAFC.

First of all, thank you for your cooperation and appreciation of the KAFC. But I have a proposal. In order to
promote its operation, I want you to inform me of the
present status on the nomination of American members.
At the 22nd meeting, I reported on the present status on
ours.

302

9. 제 24차.
   1973. 12. 7

306

지급

기 안 용 지

분류기호 문서번호	미이 723 -	(전 화 번 호)	국장 전결규정 조 항 전 결 사 항	
처 리 기 간				
시 행 일 자	73. 12. 3.		국 장	
보 존 년 한				
보조기관	과 장		협	
기 안 책 임 자	정의용	북미 2 과		
경유수신참조	수신처 참조			
제 목	SOFA 군민관계 분과위 23차 회의록 송부 및 24차 회의 개최 통보			

　　　1. 1973. 10. 30. 개최된 바 있는 제 23차 SOFA 군민관계 임시

분과위원회 회의록을 별첨 송부하오니 참고하시기 바라며,

　　　2. 동 분과위원회 제 24차 회의가 별첨과 같이 73. 12. 7. (금)

15 : 30시 미 8군 SOFA 회의실에서 개최됨을 알려드리오니 이에 대비

하시고 구 위원들은 필히 참석하여 주시기 바랍니다.

	정서
첨부 : 1. 동 회의록 1부. 　　　2. 동 의제 1부.　　끝.	
	관인
수신처 : 내무부 장관 (관리과장, 외사과장, 수 사지도 과장) 　　　　법무부 장관 (송무과장, 검찰과장) 　　　　보건사회부 장관 (만성병담당관, 마약과장) 　　　　교통부 장관 (관광국 진흥과장) 　　　　문학공보부 장관 (해외공보관 외보 과장)	발송

공통서식 1-2 (갑)
1967. 4. 4. 승인

190 mm × 268 mm (1 급인쇄용지 70g 4종)
조달청 (300,000매 인쇄)

307

청와대 정무수석 비서관 (내무. 보사담당 비서관)

국방부 장관 (민사정책 담당관)

308

AGENDA OF TWENTY-FOURTH MEETING
AD HOC SUBCOMMITTEE ON CIVIL-MILITARY RELATIONS
1530 HOURS, 7 DECEMBER 1973, US SOFA CONFERENCE ROOM

I.   Report on Developments Regarding Korean - American Friendship Councils - US Presentation.

II.   Status Reports on the Implementation of Subcommittee Recommendations - ROK and US Presentations.

III.   Consideration of Problem of Hospitalization of Korean Nationals - US and ROK Presentations.

IV.   Report on Situation in the Osan - Songtan-eup Area. US and ROK Presentations.

V.   Proposed Time for the Twenty-Fifth Ad Hoc Subcommittee Meeting, 1530 Hours, Friday 25 January 1974, ROK Capitol Building.

VI.   Adjourn.

309

공   란

공   란

공   란

공 란

공   란

공 란

공   란

공   란

공　　　　란

공 란

공   란

공 란

공　　　　란

공　　　　　란

공 란

Report to the 24th AD HOC
Sub-Committee meeting

M O H A

325

SUBJECT: IMPROVING ENVIRONMENT AROUND THE AMERICAN MILITARY BASES IN PYONGTAECK COUNTY

1. The MOHA has been, in order to encourage the people to participate in the new village movement as well as to make such a community in which US soldiers enjoy and live at ease, working on a number of projects improving environments around the US Army Units.

   As part of endeavours, the MOHA has selected Songtan-Eup in Pyongtaeck County and spent W 105,000,000 for the following projects during the past 6 months.

2. What we had done during the past 6 months are:

   * Completed projects

     o Widening and paving the roades covering an area of 190a

     o Paving the pedestrian streets covering an area of 93a

     o Building the roades covering 681 m

     o Moving for installment 12 electric poles.

     o Building 1,391 m of sewage system

     o Building 100 m of the sewage covers

     o Installing 185 street lights

     o Improving 222 poor houses

326

o Eliminating 41 poor houses

o Purchasing a night-soil disposal car

* Besides these projects, the MOHA has been working on

making greens around the compound, installing guard

rails, paving the alleys, etc.

3. Particulary, the MOHA has completed the two water work

projects with W 50,870,000 so that the people can access

to clean water.

4. Pyongtaek county government has plan to install 60 street lights

in the beginning of next year.

50
105 million

327

정/리/보/존/문/서/목/록

기록물종류	문서-일반공문서철	등록번호	17758	등록일자	2001-06-01
			7150		
분류번호	729.419	국가코드		주제	
문서철명	SOFA 한·미국 합동위원회 군민관계 임시분과위원회 - 주한미군 기지촌 현지답사 및 대책, 1974				
생산과	북미2과	생산년도	1974 - 1974	보존기간	영구
담당과(그룹)	미주	안보		서가번호	--
참조분류					
권차명					
내용목차					

마/이/크/로/필/름/사/항

촬영연도	*롤 번호	화일 번호	후레임 번호	보관함 번호
	2007-9/Re-07-10	7	1-148	

기안용지

분류기호 문서번호	미이 723 -	(전화번호　　　)	전결규정조항 장관 　전결사항	
처리기간				
시행일자	74. 5. 18.	차　관	장　관	
보존년한				

보조기관	차관보		협조	기획관리실장
	국　장			종무과장
	과　장			

기안책임자 정약용　북미2과

경유		발신		동제	
수신	내부겸재				
참조					

제　목　SOFA 군민관계 임시분과위원회의 미군 기지 현지 답사

　　1. 71. 9. 2. SOFA 군민관계임시분과위원회의 설립 이후 동

임시분과위원회는 지금 까지 25회에 걸친 주한미군 기지 및 주변 기지촌

에 대한 한.미 합동 현지 답사를 실시하여, 미군 주둔에 따른 제반 문제

해결을 통한 주둔 조건의 향상 및 한미 군민관계 개선에 기여하여 왔읍니다.

　　2. 상기 임시분과위원회는 74. 5. 3. 제 27차 회의에서 합의

(별첨 회의록 참조)한 바에 따라, 다음과 같이 금년도 첫번째의 미군 기지

에 대한 현지 답사를 실시코자 하오니 이를 재가하여 주시기 바랍니다.

　　　　　　　　　　- 다 음 -

　　가. 현지 답사 지역 : 부산 및 진해 소재 미군기지

　　나. 목　적 :

　　　　(1) 미군 기지 시찰 및 미군측 현황 청취

(2) 기지촌 지역 지방관서의 현황 청취

(3) 한미 공동 토의 및 문제점 해결 방안 강구

다. 여행 계획 :

(1) 아주 참가자 : 군민관계 임시분과위원회

한국측 위원 12명

의 장 : 외무부 북미 2과장 서기관 이 상 훈

간 사 : 외무부 북미 2과 서기관 양 세 훈

위 원 : 내무부 관리과장 서기관 전 병 우

치안국 외사과 총경 이 병 모

치안국 수사지도과 총경 유 명 두

법무부 법무실 검사 홍 유 택

법무부 검찰과 검사 신 창 언

교통부 관광진흥과장 서기관 김 철 용

보사부 만성병과장 서기관 오 영 일

보사부 마약과장 서기관 이 희 찬

문공부 외보과장 서기관 김 광 식 X

국방부 민사과장 대령 심 용 순

(2) 여행기간 : 74. 5. 28. - 30. (2박 3일)

(3) 이용 편 :

(가) 서울 - 부산간 : 항공 왕복

(나) 부산 - 진해간 : 버스 왕복

(4) 경비 지출 근거 : 일반외교비 국내여비 (SOFA 운영)

첨부 : 동 협의록 1부. 끝.

3

공 란

공   란

공   란

공　　　란

공 란

공　　　란

공 란

공   란

기 안 용 지

분류기호 문서번호	미이 723 -	(전화번호)	전 결 규 정 조 항 국 장 전 결 사 항
처 리 기 간			
시 행 일 자	74. 5. 21.		국 장
보 존 년 한			
보조기관	과 장		협
기 안 책 임 자	정의용 북미 2과		
경 유		발	
수 신 참 조	수신처 참조	신	
제 목	SOFA 군민관계 임시분 과위원회의 기지촌 현지 답사 계획 통보		

발 No. 21387
1974. 5. 22
외무부
검 열

74. 5. 3. SOFA 군민관계임시분 과위원회 제 27차 회의에서 합의
된 바에 따라, 다음과 같이 금년도 첫번째의 미군 기지 및 주변 기지촌에
대한 한.미합동 현지 답사를 실시 예정이니 각 위원들은 필히 참석하기
바랍니다.

- 다 음 -

1. 답사지역 : 부산 및 진해 소재 미군 기지
2. 목   적 :
  가. 미군 기지 시찰 및 미군측 현황 정취
  나. 기지촌 지역 지방 관서의 현황 정취
  다. 한미공동 토의 및 문제점 해결 방안 강구
3. 여행계획 :
  가. 참가자 : 군민관계임시분 과위원회 위원
  나. 기 간 : 74. 5. 28. - 30.

정서

관인

발송

0201-1-8A (갑)
1969. 11. 10 승인

190mm×268mm (특급인쇄용지40g/m²)
조 달 청 (1,000,000매 인 쇄)

다. 이용편 : 항공편

라. 여 비 : 외무부 부담.

4. 세부일정 : 추후 통보

끝.

수신처 : 내무부 장관 (관리과장, 외사과장, 수사지도 과장)

법무부 장관 (송무과장, 검찰과장)

교통부 장관 (관광국진흥과장)

보건사회부 장관 (만성병과장, 마약과장)

문화공보부 장관 (해외공보관 외보 과장)

국방부 장관 (비상계획관실 민사정책담당관)

0201—1—43A (2—2)
1972. 12. 29 승 인

190mm×263mm (특급인쇄용지 40g/m²)
조 달 청 (2,000,000매 인 쇄)

기 안 용 지

분류기호 문서번호	미이 723 -	(전화번호)	전 결 규 정 조 항 **국장** 전 결 사 항		
처리기간	**지급**				
시행일자	74. 5. 25.				
보존년한			국 장		

보 조 기 관	과 장	ㅈ		협 조	

기안책임자	정 의 용	북미 2과		
경 유				통
수 신	수신처 참조			
참 조				제
제 목	SOFA 군민관계 임시분과위원회 현지 답사			

연 : 미이 723 - 21387 (74. 5. 22.)

　　1. 연호로 통보한 부산 및 진해 소재 미군 기지에 대한 군민관계 임시분과위원회의 현지 답사 계획은 미측 사정으로 인하여 당분간 연기 되었으며, 동 일정은 추후 확정되는데로 통보하겠읍니다.

　　2. 상기 일정의 연기에 따라 74. 5. 30. (목) 의정부 소재 미군 기지에 대하여 금년도 첫번째 현지 답사를 실시 예정이니 각 위원들은 필히 참석바라며, 동일 12:40시까지 중앙청 동편 주차장으로 집합하기 바랍니다.

첨부 : 의정부 현지 답사 일정 1부.　　　　　끝.

수신처 : 내무부 장관 (관리과장, 외사과장, 수사지도 과장)

　　　　 법무부 장관 (송무 과장, 검찰 과장)

	정 서
	관 인
	발 송

교통부 장관 (관광국 진흥 과장)

보건사회부 장관 (만성병과장, 마약과장)

문학공보부장관 (해외공보관 외보 과장)

국방부 장관 (비상계획관실 민사정책담당관)

15

0201—1—43A (2—2)
1972. 12. 29 승 인

190mm×268mm (무급인쇄용지 40g/m²)
조 달 청 (2,000,000매 인 쇄)

Schedule for trip to Uijongbu
(30 May 197X)

2. A tentative schedule for this trip is as follows:

1230 ~~1300~~	Bus departs parking lot adjacent to Theater #2 for drive to
~~1245~~ ~~Enroute~~	Uijongbu
1400-1430	Arrive HQ I Corps, (ROK/US)Gp Conference Room
	Refreshments
1430-1440	Introductory remarks by representative of Commander,
	LTG Hollingsworth
1440-1530	Civil affairs and associated presentations
	Provost Marshal
	Surgeon
	Drugs and race relations
1530-1540	Break
1540-1630	ROK officials presentations
1630-1700	Open discussion
1700-1800	Bus to O-Club, Dinner
1800-1815	Bus downtown to club area
1815-1915	Visit tourist establishments
1930-2100	Return to Seoul.

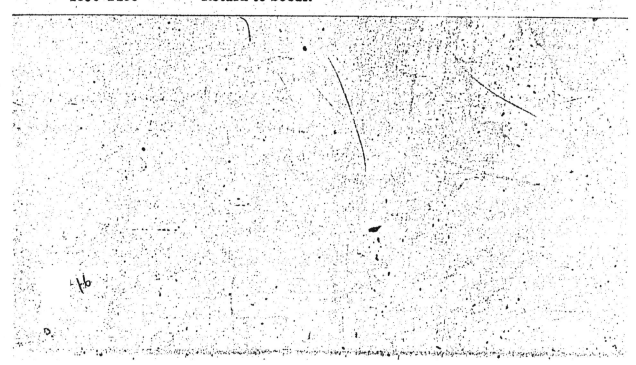

Proposed Trip to Chinhae/Pusan by the Ad Hoc Subcommittee on Civil-Military
Relations

28 May 1974

0945 - 1015	US Component Enroute to Kimpo International Airport
1030 - 1130	Fly Seoul to Chinhae
1145 - 1200	Bus to Dining Hall
1200 - 1245	Lunch at Chinhae
1245 - 1300	Bus to HQ (?) Conference Room
1300 - 1500	Conference
1500 - 1530	Bus to Masan - See Turtleboat Monument
1630 - 1800	Bus to Pusan, Check in Hotel _____
1900	Dinner at Hotel _____

29 May 1974

0800	Breakfast at Hotel _____
0845 - 0900	Bus to Hialeah Compound
0900 - 1200	Conference
1200 - 1300	Lunch at Hialeah Compound
1300 - 1500	~~Open (?)~~ PUSAN CITY HALL
1500 - 1515	Bus to Airport
1530 - 1630	Fly Pusan to Kimpo
1645 - 1700	Bus to Yongsan

공   란

전　통　문

해보 1731 - 528

수 신 : 외무부 장관

참 조 : 미주국장

발 신 : 문공부 장관

제 목 : SOFA 군민관계 임시분 과위원회의 기지촌 현지 답사

내 용 : 1. 미이 723 - 21387 (74. 5. 22.) 및 미이 723 - 22053
　　　　　　(74. 5. 25.) 관련입니다.

　　　　　2. 당부 SOFA 군민관계 임시분 과위원회위원 (김광식)은
　　　　　　6. 2.까지 출장으로 5. 30.(목) 의정부 소재 미군기지
　　　　　　현지 답사에 참석치 못하게 됨을 통고합니다.

수화자 : 정 의 용

송화자 : 박희두

통화시간 : 12:00

SOFA 군민관계 임시분과위원회의 기지촌 현지답사 결과보고

1. 일   시: 1974. 5. 30. (목) 1230 - 2100

2. 답사지역: 경기도 의정부시 소재 한미 1군단 지역

3. 참 가 자: 한국측: 외무부 북미 2과장 (한국측의장) 외 10명
              미군측: 주한미군 민사처장 (미측의장) 외 7명

4. 주요 토의 내용:

   가.   사격장 무단출입 (Range Encroachment) 문제

      (1)   1군단 산하 미군 사격장에 고철 수집을 위하여 민간인이
            무단 출입함으로써 상당수의 사상자가 지속 발생하고
            있으며, 이로 인한 사격 훈련의 막대한 지장으로 말미
            암아 미군의 전투력이 저하되는 결과를 초래하고 있음.

      (2)   동 문제 해결을 위한 한국정부의 강력한 조치를 요청함.

   나.   기타 군민관계 문제

      성병, 마약, 인종문제등은 의정부시를 비롯한 한국측 관계관과의
      협조가 원만하게 이루어지고 있어 다른 지역에 비해 별 문제가
      없음.

5.   조치사항:

   5. 31. 내무부 치안국에서는 사격장 무단출입 문제와 관련하여 현지에
   조사단을 파견하였으며, 동 조사 결과에 따라 관계부처와의 협의를
   통하여 문제 해결책을 강구할것임.

북미2과	양교재	74년 5월 일	담당	과장	국장	차관보	차관	장관

20

1974. 5. 30.

기지촌 대책 현황

의 정 부 시

21

목 차

~/~

기지촌 대책 일반현황

1. 사업 내역

가. 사회 대책

- 질서 확립

- 군수품 도난 · 암거래 근절

- 인종차별 배제

- 윤락 여성 선도 —

나. 보건 대책

- 성병예방 및 치료

- 마약 및 습관성 의약품 단속

- 판광업소 위생대책

- 청소 강화

- 결핵 예방 및 치료

다. 환경 정화 대책

- 도로 및 상하수도 시설

- 보안등 및 가로등 시설

- 도로변 미화 가로수 식재

~2~

23

o 불량주택 및 간판 정리

라 친선 활동 전개

o 한미 친선

o 홍보 활동

마 생활 기반 조성

o 영세민 구호

o 직업 보도 및 훈련

o 도시 새마을 사업. 강력추진

2 73년도 사업 실적

o 성병 관리소 1동 (106평) 신축

o 가드레일 4.524㎞ 시설

o 가로수 600본 식재

o 하수도 10.264㎞ 시설

o 도로 축조 및 보수 11.941㎞ 완료

o 치수 사업 11.508㎡ 완료

o 가로등 보안등 유지 보수등 57개 사업을 완수

-3~

3. 74년도 계획대 실적 (5월말 현재)

가. 사회 보건 대책

o 윤락여성 성병 접진 : 년 70,000 명 계획에

29,000 명 실시

o 윤락여성 선도 및 교양강좌 · 년간 4회 계획에

1회 실시

o 판광업소 위생검사 : 년 4회에 1회 실시

o 불량업소 시설 개수 : 3개소 계획에 1개소 개수

(전업소 6, 10한 시설개수 지시)

o 습판성 마약 합동단속 결핵 예방 청소사업등 9개

사업을 강력 추진

나. 환경 정화 대책

o 도로 포장 : 3건 177a 완료 (100%)

o 보도 부럭 : 4건 22a 완료 (100%)

o 하수도 복개 : 1개소 300m (6월 발주)

o 보안등 설책 · 10등 설치 및 가로등 유지관리

계획대로 완료

-4-

25

○　불량주택 및 간판정비 60동. 외에 12건의 환경정화

　　사업 추진

다　한미 친선 활동대책

　○　한미 친선 : 면 6회중 2회 분과 위원회 3회실시

　※　매원 하사관단을 招致하여 좌담회를 통한

　　한국 소개

라.　생활 기반 조성 대책

　○　기지촌 영세민 928 명에 대한 부상구호 및 화재구호

실시

~5~

26.

성병관리현황

1. 72년도 검진 및 치료 실적

※ 대응 성병 진료소　　　　　　　〈 72.1월 ~ 12월말 〉

검진 연인원	낙 검 내 역						치 료	
	총 계	%	임 질	%	W.B.C	%	인 원	%
63,896	748	1.1	219	0.3	529	0.8	635	84

2. 73년 검진 및 치료 실적

※ 대응 성병 진료소　　　　　　　〈 73년 1월 ~ 5월말까지 〉

검진 연인원	낙 검 내 역						치 료	
	총 계	%	임 질	%	W.B.C	%	인 원	%
22,873	422	1.8	259	1.1	163	0.7	346	82

3. 관영화 이후 검진 및 치료 실적

〈 73. 6월 ~ 12월 〉

월별	검진대상	수진연인원	낙 검 내 역						치 료	
			총 계	%	임 질	%	W.B.C	%	인 원	%
총 계	25,319	22,039	2,251	10.7	1,003	4.7	1,248	5.4	2,095	96
6	3,200	2,830	351	12.4	153	5.4	198	6.9	333	95
7	3,587	3,106	338	10.0	139	4.4	199	6.3	321	95
8	3,820	3,534	340	9.6	114	3.2	226	6.4	316	96
9	3,533	3,149	330	10.4	132	4.1	198	6.2	310	94
10	3,747	3,130	286	9.4	145	4.7	141	4.5	281	95
11	3,826	3,210	322	10.0	158	4.8	164	5.1	312	97
12	3,204	3,080	274	8.9	152	4.9	122	3.9	222	94

~6~

ㅂ. 74년도 검진 및 치료실적

(74. 1월 ~ 4월말)

연번	검진대상	수검연인원	나 검 내 역						치 료	
			총계	%	임질	%	WBC	%	인원	%
1	3277	3095	333	10.7	163	5.3	170	5.0	309	93
2	2970	2691	318	11.8	187	6.9	131	4.9	311	98
3	3444	3123	264	8.2	160	5.0	104	3.2	253	96
4	3492	3125	342	10.9	231	7.4	111	3.0	314	92

※ 매 독

73년. 6월 ~ 12월말

대 상 인 원	수 검 인 원	양 성 자	%	비 고
2,400	2,198	165	7.5	73년 3차 실시

74년 1/4 분기

대 상 인 원	수 검 인 원	양 성 자	%	비 고
750	736	39	5.2	74년 1차 실시

※ 일반 접객 업소

74. 4. 15 ~ 5. 28 현재.

등 록 인 원	수 검 연인원	보 균 자	%	비 고
182	335	8	2.4	2주1회(금요일)

~4~

마약 사범 단속 상황

년도별	마약 사범		습관성 의약품		비 고
	단 속	구속 처리	단 속	구속 처리	
계	20 건	16 건	333 건	199 건	
1973년	18	14	276	158	
1974년별	2	2	57	41	

~8~

29

업소 방문 계획

방문순서	업소명	소 재 지	방문시간	소요시간	비 고
1	아리랑 홀	가능 2동	18:20~18:30	10분	
2	백운크럽	"	18:30~18:40	"	
3	칠성홀	"	18:40~18:50	"	
4	앤젤다방	의정부1동	19:00~19:10	"	
5	잠보다방	"	19:10~19:20	"	
6	늘봄다방	"	19:20~19:30	"	
7	999	"	19:30~19:40	"	

~9~

3°

****

STATUS OF CAMP VILLAGE CONTROL

****

30 MAY 1974

CITY OF UIJONGBU

31

CONTENTS

- 1 -

32

```
┌─────────────────────────────────────────────────┐
│ I.  GENERAL STATUS OF CAMP VILLAGE CONTROL        │
└─────────────────────────────────────────────────┘
```

1. PROJECTS

    a. SOCIAL CONTROL

        MAINTENANCE OF SOCIAL ORDER

        ERADICATION OF MILITARY SUPPLY THEFT & BLACK-MARKETING

        ELIMINATION OF RACIAL DISCRIMIATION

        PROPER GUIDANC OF BUSINESS GIRLS

    b. HEALTH CONTROL

        PREVENTION & TREATMENT OF V.D.

        CONTROL OF NARCOTICS & HABITUAL DRUGS.

        SANITARY CONTROL OF TOURIST ESTABLISHMENTS.

        INTENSIFIED AREA CLEANING.

        PREVENTION & TREATMENT OF TB.

    c. ENVIRONMENTAL PURIFICATION

        CONSTRUCTION OF ROAD, WATER SUPPLY SYSTEM & SEWER.

        INSTALLATION OF SECURITY & STREET LIGHTS.

        ROAD-SIDE BEAUTIFICATION & TREE PLANTING.

        ADJUSTMENT OF POOR CONDITIONED HOUSES & COMMERCIAL SIGNS

- 2 -

33

d. FRIENDSHIP ACTIVITIES.

KOREAN-AMERICAN FRIENDSHIP COUNCIL MEETINGS.

PUBLIC INFORMATION ACTIVITIES.

e. CREATION OF LIVELIHOOD FOUNDATION

RELIEF OF POOR PEOPLE.

VOCATIONAL GUIDANCE & TRAINING.

INTENSIFIED ROAD AREA SAE-MAUL MOVEMENT.

ACHIEVEMENTS IN CY '73

CONSTRUCTION OF A NEW V.D. CLINIC

SIDE-WALK RAIL: 4,524m.

STREET TREES: 600 ea.

SEWER: 10,264m.

UP-GRADING & MAINTENANCE OF ROAD: 11,941m.

FLOOD CONTROL: 11,508m2.

SECURITY & STREET LIGHTS: 57.

- 3 -

34

3. PROGRESS IN CY '75 (AS OF END OF MAY)

    a. SOCIAL & HEALTH.

        MEDICAL EXAMINATION ON BUSINESS GIRLS (BG) 29,000 COMPLETED
        OUT OF 70,000 ANTICIPATED YEAR.

        PROPER GUIDANCE & EDUCATION OF BG: COMPLETED ONCE OUT OF
        4 TIMES A YEAR.

        SANITARY INSPECTION: CONDUCTED ONCE OUT OF 4 TIMES PLANED.
        (ONCE QUARTERLY).

        IMPROVEMENT OF UNSATISFACTORY ESTABLISHMENTS COMPLETED ONCE
          .... OUT OF 3 PLANED.

        CONSTANT EFFORTS ARE BEING MADE ON 9 PROJECTS TO INCLUDE
        JOINT CONTROL OF NARCOTICS, PREVENTON OF TB, AREA CLEANING.

    b. ENVIRONMENTAL PURIFICATION

ROAD PAVEMENT:	3 CASES	177a	(100%)
SIDE-WALK BLOCK:	4 CASES	22a	(100%)
COVERAGE OF SEWER:		300m	(TO BE COMMENCED IN JUNE)

        PPLACEMENT OF 10 SECURITY LIGHTS COMPLETED AS PLANED.

        IMPROVEMENT OF POOR CONTIONED HOUSES & COMMERCIAL SIGNS:
        60 HOUSES & ENVIRONMENTAL PURIFICATION WORKS OF 12 CASES
        ON THE WAY.

    c. FRIENDSHIP ACTIVITIES: KAFC MEETING: TWICE OUT OF 6 MEETINGS
        & 3 SUB-COMMITTEE MEETINGS CONDUCTED.

        INVITATION OF US NCO's ON INTRODUCTORY TOURS COMPLTED 3 TIMES
        OUT OF 6 PLANED.

    d. CREATION OF LIVELIHOOD FOUNDATION: RELIEF AND EMPLOYMENT OF
        928 POOR PEOPLE.

- 4 -

35

1. GC EXAM (BY CONTRACT PROVATE CLINICS (CPC)) & TREATMENT IN CY'72

TOTAL EXAMINED	EXAM REJETEES						TREATMENT	
	TOTAL	%	GC	%	WBC +4	%	NO OF PERSONS	%
63,896	748	1.1	219	0.3	529	0.8	635	84

2. GC EXAM (BY CPC) & TREATMENT IN CY'73

TOTAL EXAMINED	EXAM REJECTEES						TREATMENT	
	TOTAL	%	GC	%	WBC +4	%	NO OF PERSONS	%
22,873	422	1.8	259	1.1	163	0.7	346	82

3. STATISTICS OF EC EXAM & TREATMENT SINCE THE WORK WAS TRANSFERRED TO PUBLIC HEALTH CENTER (VD CLINIC)

JUNE – DEC '73

MO	NO OF ELIGI	NO OF EXAM	EXAM REJECTEES						TREATMENT	
			TOTAL	%	GC	%	WBC+4	%	NO OF PERSONS	%
TOTAL	25,319	22,039	2,251	10.2	1,003	4.7	1,248	5.4	2,095	96
JUNE	3,200	2,830	351	12.4	153	5.4	198	6.9	333	95
JULY	3,587	3,106	338	10.0	139	4.4	199	6.3	321	95
AUG	3,820	3,534	340	9.6	114	3.2	226	6.4	316	96
SEPT	3,522	3,149	330	10.4	132	4.1	198	6.2	310	94
OCT	3,749	3,130	296	9.4	155	4.9	141	4.5	281	95
NOV	3,826	3,210	322	10.0	158	4.8	164	5.1	312	97
DEC	3,604	3,080	274	8.9	152	4.9	122	3.9	222	94

- 5 -

4. EXAM & TREATMENT IN CY'74

MO	NO OF ELIGI	TOTAL EXAM	EXAM REJECTED						TREATMENT	
			TOTAL	%	GC	%	VBC+L	%	NO PERSONS	%
JAN	3,277	3,095	333	10.7	163	5.3	170	5.6	309	93
FEB	2,970	2,691	318	11.8	187	6.9	131	4.9	311	98
MAR	3,444	3,128	264	8.2	160	5.0	104	3.2	253	96
APR	3,492	3,125	342	10.9	231	7.4	111	3.0	314	92

5. SYPHILIS

NO OF ELIGIBILITY	NO EXAMINED	POSTVE	%	REMARKS
2,400	2,198	165	7.5	

NO OF ELIGIBILITY	NO EXAMINED	POSTVE	%	REMARKS
750	736	39	5.2	

6. LOCAL ENTERTAINERS' (GC)

NO REGISTERED	TOTAL EXAMINED	POSTVE	%	REMARKS
182	335	78	24	Once every Two Weeks

-- 6 --

34

III. NARCOTIC CONTROL

YEAR	NARCOTIC		HABITUAL DRUGS		REMARKS
	NO CHECKED	ARRESTED	NO CHECKED	ARRESTED	
TOTAL	20 Cases	16 Cases	333 Cases	199 Cases	
CY '73	18 "	14 "	276 "	158 "	
CY '74	2 "	2 "	57 "	41 "	

IV ITINERARY

FOR VIST TO LOCAL AREA

TIME	ACTIVITY	
1. 1820 – 1830	VISIT TO ARIRANG CLUB	
2. 1830 – 1840	" BAIK-UN CLUB	NEAR BY JACKSON CIRCLE.
3. 1840 – 1850	" 7th STAR CLUB	
4. 1900 – 1910	" ANGEL TEA ROOM	
5. 1910 – 1920	" JUMBO TEA ROOM	DOWN-TOWN
6. 1920 – 1930	" NEUL BOM TEA ROOM	UIJONGBU
7. 1930 – 1940	" 999 BAR	

AD HOC SUBCOMMITTEE
CIVIL-MILITARY RELATIONS

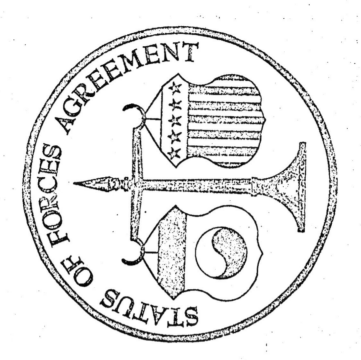

STATUS OF FORCES AGREEMENT

VISIT TO UIJONGBU CITY
I CORPS (ROK/US) GROUP
30 MAY 1974

SCHEDULE

Time	Activity
1230 – 1400	Bus departs Yongsan Theater #2 lot, Route via American Embassy and Capitol Building
1400 – 1430	Arrive HQ I Corps (ROK/US) Group Refreshments
1430 – 1440	Introductory remarks by LTG Hollingsworth, Commander, I Corps (ROK/US) Group

US Presentations

1440 – 1500	Range Encroachment
1500 – 1515	Anti VD Program
1515 – 1525	People-to-People Activities
1525 – 1535	Race Relations/Drugs/Law Enforcement Program
1535 – 1545	Break

ROK Presentations

1545 – 1635	Presentations by ROK Component and Officials of the City of Uijongbu
1635 – 1700	Free Discussion Period
1700 – 1800	Dinner
1800 – 1810	Bus to Downtown Club Area
1810 – 1930	Visit Tourist Establishments
1930 – 2100	Return to Seoul

NOTE: Dinner this evening will be your choice of Prime Rib of Beef, or Cordon Bleu.

Representing the Republic of Korea Component

Mr. LEE Sang Hoon
Mr. JEON Byoung Woo
Mr. YOO Myong Doo
LTC KOH Byung Soo
Mr. KIM Chol Yong
Mr. OH Young Il
Mr. LEE Hi Chan
Mr. LEE Byoung Mo
Mr. YANG Sei Hoon
Mr. CHUNG Eui Yong

Representing the United States Component

Captain W. E. Sharp, USN
Colonel W. A. Zeigler, USA
Lt Colonel Richard Singleton, USA
Lt Colonel Paul V. Colaianni, USAF
Major W. E. Schmidt, USAF
Mr. John S. Boardman, American Embassy
Mr. MUN Chae Sik, Community Relations Officer, PAO
Mr. AN Chang Hun, USFK (Interpreter)

Representing the City of Uijongbu

Mayor MIN, C. K.
Prosecutor PARK, J. G.
Superintendent IN, K. K.
Mr. KIM, B. M., Mayor's Asst for Community Relations

Representing I Corps (ROK/US) Group

Colonel Porcher L. Taylor, CDR, I Corps (ROK/US) Group (Rear Area)
Colonel Kenneth F. Myfelt, G1, I Corps (ROK/US) Group

나

AD HOC SUBCOMMITTEE
CIVIL-MILITARY RELATIONS

STATUS OF FORCES AGREEMENT

VISIT TO PUSAN AND CHINHAE
18-19 JUNE 1974

42

SCHEDULE OF TRIP TO PUSAN/CHINHAE

18 June 1974

Time	Activity
0800-0845	Bus Departs ROK Capitol Building for Kimpo
0930-1100	Fly to Pusan in Command T-29 Bus to Hialeah Compound
1130-1230	Lunch at Officers' Open Mess with Representatives of 2d Transp. Gp and the City of Pusan. Welcome by Commander, 2d Transp. Gp, COL Thomas E. Benson, USA
1245-1430	Presentations by Officials of the City of Pusan and the 2d Transp. Gp.
1445-1745	Tour of Pusan and Surrounding Area and Inspection of Entertainment Establishments.
1800-1815	Check in at Hotels
1900-2030	Dinner

19 June 1974

Time	Activity
1000-1005	Bus departs Hotel for Pusan Airport
1030-1100	Fly to Chinhae
1130-1230	Welcome by Commanding Officer, Naval Forces Component, Chinhae, and Mayor of the City of Chinhae
1230-1330	Lunch at USN Mess with Representatives of the USN Component and Officials of the City of Chinhae
1345-1530	Tour of Chinhae Area
1600-1730	Fly to Kimpo Intern'l Airport, Seoul
1745-1830	Bus to Yongsan Garrison via ROK Capitol Bldg. and Post Office Outside Gate #19.

Representing the Republic of Korea Component

Mr. LEE Sang Hoon
Mr. YANG Sei Hoon
Mr. JEON Byoung Woo
Mr. LEE Byung Mo
Mr. HONG Yue Taek
Mr. KIM Chol Yong
Mr. OH Young Il
COL SIM Yong Soon

Representing the United States Component

CAPT Wallace E. Sharp, USN
COL Louis E. Herrick, USAF
COL John D. Granger, USA
COL William W. Woodside, USA
LTC Robert D. Haines, USAF
MAJ Walter E. Schmidt, USAF
Mr. AN Chang Hun, USFK Interpreter
Mr. Blanchard K. Parsons*

*Mr. Parsons (FSIO-4) is the resident USIS Representative in Pusan. He will join our group there and represent the AMEMB in our discussions.

Sequence of Events on Special KAFC Meeting: 1245-1430 hrs, 18 June 74,
특별 한미친선 위원회 회의순   Pusan Officers Open Mess

Attendees: All US & ROK members of KAFC and Ad Hoc Subcommittee on
           Civil-Military Relations.
참석인   부산 한미친선위원회 회원 및 행협한미관계 분과위원회 전원

1. Opening Remarks: Col Benson and Mayor Park
   개회사   베슨 사령관 및 박시장
2. Introduction of KAFC and Ad Hoc Subcommittee Members
   참석회원 소개
3. Old and New Business:
   신규 사항
   a. Local Community and Governmental Relations and People to People
      한미정부관계 및 군민관계 사업 (10분)
      Program(10 minutes)....................... Mr. Yoo, Civil Affairs
                                                미사처 유 영복 씨
   b. Cultural Exchanges(10 minutes)............... Mr. Parsons, American
      문화교류 (10분)   Cultural Center
                                                미국 문화원 원장 파-슨즈 씨
   c. Korean National Police - US Military Cooperation and Coordination:
      한미경찰 협조사항 (마약단속, 절도, 암거래, 성병단속, 10분)
      Narcotics and Drug Control, Larceny and Blankmarketing and Vice

      Control(10 minutes)....................... Capt Welling
                                                웰링 대위
   d. Health & Sanitation(10 minutes).............. Maj Cederburg
      보건위생(10분)   서더버거 소령
   e. Presentation by city representatives(20 minutes)... Mr. Shin, City PIO
      시 공보실장 및 보사국장 (20분)   Chief and Mr. Kang, City
                                                Health & Welfare Bureau

   f. Presentation by US Chairman, Ad Hoc Subcommittee on CM Relations
      (5 minutes) 행협 한미관계 분과위원회 미측의장 (5분)

   g. Presentation by ROK Chairman, Ad Hoc Subcommittee on CM Relations
      (5 minutes) 행협 한미관계 분과위원회 한국측 의장 (5분)

4. Free Discussion by All Present(25 minutes)
   자유토론 (전원, 25분)
5. Showing of a 20-minute documentary on city tourism
   시 관광영화 상영 (20분)
6. Closing Remarks by Commander, 2d Trans Gp
   폐회사, 베슨 사령관

74 基地村 淨化對策

釜山直轄市

45

14. 基地村 環境 整備 事業

1. 目 標

가. 基地村 周辺의 各種 社会悪을 根絶

나. 性病과 痲藥을 根絶하고 施設을 改善하여 外国
人에게 健全한 休息処를 提供

다. 輪落女性에게 敎養講座와 職業 輔導 訓練을 実
施하여 資質을 높이고 観光 要員으로서 矜持
와 自頁心을 갖도록 指導

라. 基地 周辺의 環境을 整備하여 깨끗한 거리를
造成

마. 韓美 親善活動을 强化하기 위하여 韓美 公
益 委員会 会議를 開催

―1―

가. 保健 對策

(單位 : 千원)

事業名		目標	實績	事業費	備考
1. 性病予防治療	檢診	目標 22,100名	目 11,525	8,776	대상 300名
	治療	目 2,200名	927		
2. 麻藥및 習慣性 医藥品 團束	單美合同團束	50回	36回	813	
	臨時團束	30回	31回		
3. 觀光業所 衛生對策	衛生檢査 1개10所 4回	年68回	年34回		
	健康診斷 1개10所 2回	年600名	年280名	비예산	
	敎養敎育 1개10所 4回	4回 1,200名	2回 560名		

4. 淸掃强化	塵芥차량 配置	4台	每日 4台		진개 분뇨를 100% 收去
	手車	4台	4台	13.084	깨끗한 거
	분立 收去車	2台	2台		리 환경조성
5. 結核予防	X-線 檢診	550名	196名	32	1
	객담 檢診	300名	55名		

-3-

40

4. 社會環境 韓美 親善事業

區 分	事業名	目 標	実績	事業費	備 考
社会淨化 對策	耳需品절도 및 暗去来 團束	3個班編成 (18名) 毎日2回團束		888	
	倫落女性 善導	敎養 講座 2回 12回 職業 輔導 訓練 對象 200名 6日 교육 쿠가 교회	400名 35名	18	
環境淨化 對策 事業	새마을建設 事業	1.下水溝改修 工事 L=320m			入札施行中

		、B = 70 CM		
		2. 道路鋪裝 工事	151,000	65棟 철거 잡질중
		L = 650 m		
		B = 25 m		
韓美親善 活 動	韓美親善 協議会運営	協議会開催 2回		80
		4回		
計				172,691

— 5 —

ㅂ

韓美 親善. 協議會運営

- 7 -

51

韓美親善 協議會名單

o 韓國側

委員長　釜山市長　　　　　　　　　　　　朴英秀

委　員　釜山市西區西大新洞3가279
　　　　釜山市政諮問委員長　　　　　　　姜在鎬

　　　　釜山市 中區 大橋洞2가38
　　　　釜山市觀光協会長　　　　　　　　王指穀

　　　　株式会社東洋테레비죤釜山放送局
　　　　　　社　長　　　　　　　　　　　金漠基

　　　　釜山市 中區 光復洞 1가6
　　　　釜山國際婦人会長　　　　　　　　金慧星

　　　　釜山市 警察局長　　　　　　　　　姜斗鉉

　　　　釜山市 保健社会局長　　　　　　　裵判守

幹　事　釜山市 文化公報室長　　　　　　　辛容官

-9-

52

1. 韓美 親善 協議会 発足에 対한 経過

(1). 発足 日時 : 1953. 7. 27

(2). 名　　稱 : 韓美 公益 委員会

(3). 当時 両側 代表

　　○ 韓国側 : 第4代 梁聖奉 慶南 知事

　　○ 美国側 : 美釜山基地司令官 힛트라 准將

(4). 63. 1. 1 釜山市가 政府 直轄市로 昇格 됨에 따라 第12代 金玄玉 市長 在任時 釜山市로 移管

(5). 1972. 1 부터 韓美 親善 委員会로 그 名稱을 変更

(6). 1973. 6. 22 内務部長官의 指示에 依拠 韓美 親善 協議会로 名稱 変更

(7). 発足 事由

　　○ 1953. 7. 27 韓国 動乱 休戦会談 署名 即后 地方 韓美間의 友好 増進및 紐帯 強化

　　○ 文化 芸術 交流 및 各種 事業 行事 文援

2. 韓美 親善 協議会 設置 條例制定

　　　　(73. 7. 28)

3. 韓·美 親善 協議会 運営 要綱

　(1). 目 的

　　　　美国의 経済的 支援만을 받아내는 機構라는

　　　　從来의 그릇된 認識으로 부터 自立 対等한

　　　　協議体로 発展시켜 両国間에 相互 協助와

　　　　親善의 四謀로서 駐韓 美軍의 올바른 韓国観

　　　　을 定立시키고 両国의 細帶를 強化코자 새로

　　　　의 委員会를 構成 運営

　(2). 設置 部署

　　　　우리 領土内에 駐屯하고 있는 全 美陸海空軍部

　　　　隊를 対象으로 하여 設置

　(3). 名 稱 : 韓美 親善 協議会

　(4). 技 能

　　　　　　　　　　　　　　-//-

54

○ 相互間에 理解의 增進과 親善의 圖謀로써
  國威를 宣揚

○ 兩側의 衝突事故 未然 防止

○ 提起된 問題는 理解와 友誼로써 充分한 對話
  를 通하여 合意하고 調整하는 雰圍気
  調整

⑤ 備成

○ 委員数는 兩側이 同数로 함

○ 美軍側도 部隊長을 委員長으로 參謀를 委員으
  로 하여 別途 協議会를 構成

○ 委員長은 委員의 選任時 委嘱狀을 解任時는
  解任 通知書를 交付

⑥ 会合

○ 会合은 月/回 定期로 開催하되 最初会議에
  서 時日을 指定

o 会合 相互 交代로 開催하여 附設案件이 없드라도

  親善圖謀를 為하여 반드시 開催

o 会議場은 主催側의 施設物을 利用하고 主催側이 準備

o 椅子의 配列은 兩側委員長을 中心으로 左右에 兩

  側委員들이 2列 配置

o 会議 参席時는 可能限한 正服을 着用하고 言行에

  신중을 기하여 相対方 議長의 品位 維持

(7) 参考人의 出席

  附設案件의 內容에 따라 参考人 (関係人)의 出席

  発言이나 物証 提示

(8) 公報 (発表文)

  協議会開催 結果를 公表코자 할때는 事前에 兩側

  이 合意를 거쳐 発表

(9) 報告

  本協議会 開催狀況을 內務部長官에게 報告

~3~

5b

10. 既存委員会의 閉止

이 規定에 依하여 設置되지 아니한 既存의 各種

委員会나 類似 団体는 全部 本 協議会에 統合되든

閉止

4. 韓美親善協議会 運営状況

가 会議開催実績

年度別	実績	備　　　　　考
72年度	5回	第148次 ~ 第152次
73 "	5 "	153 ~ 157
74 "	2 "	158 ~ 159
計	12回	

나 主要行事

(1) 文化交流

○ 毎年 7月28日을 韓美親善의 날로 制定

(73. 5. 4)

o 韓国팀과 美側팀 61回 親善競技

o 国際婦人会 等 總 34回 親善行事 開催

o 韓国側에서 美軍의 営外家族이 所持하는 T.V 視
  聽料 免除措置

(2) 厚生

o 72. 9. 14 暴雨時 羅災民 救護用 600余名 分의
  食糧및 寝具衣類를 支援 받음

o 孤児院및 厚生施設 24個所에 装備支援 받음
  (1.344 時間)

(3) 保健衛生

o 医療事業으로 국민患者 延 260名의 無料治療
  와 170名의 無料手術

(4) 消防

o 火災時 62回의 消防支援을 받음

o 消防을 為한 訓練및 세미나 實施에 相互協助

~5~

58

~16~

(5) 警察

ㅇ 麻藥 窃盜 軍需物資 不正取扱 暗去来 等

公安 秩序 維持에 警察과 緊密한 協助

(6) 새마을 資材支援

ㅇ 釜山鎮区 金谷荷 姉妹 結緣 拡声栈 襲栈具

(約 50万원 相当) 및 医療品 等을 支援받음

ㅇ 影島区 青鶴洞 外 2個洞의 마을 文庫에 多数

의 册字와 음반 25 枚 寄贈

ㅇ 새마을 事業用 資材 油紙 609 롤지 石骨板

429 枚 支援 받음

(7) 観光

ㅇ 74. 5. 7에 美 7 艦隊 所属 미드웨이호 및

오크라호마 등等 観光 寄港時 全市民의

歡迎

(8) 其他

ㅇ 両側 相互間의 必要時는 協助 調整

韓美親善協議會設置條例

~17~

-60

1973년 7월 26일

부 산 시 장

부산시 한미친선 협의회 설치조례 제 707 호

제 1 조 (목적) 이 조례는 부산시 한미친선협의회 (이
하 "협의회" 라 한다)의 설치와 운영에 관한
사항을 규정함을 목적으로 한다

제 2 조 (설치) 주한 재부 미군과 지역사회간의 올바른
이해촉진 및 우의증진으로 상호 협조 및 유대 강
화를 위하여 협의를 둔다

제 3 조 (기능) ① 협의회는 주한미군과 지역사회간의 공
동 관심사와 양측에 활성 또는 발생의 우려가
있는 제반 사항에 대하여 상호간의 이해 협조로서
적절한 대책을 강구하고 조정하며 제기된 문제를 양 측
의 합의로서 해결한다

② 전항의 공동관심사는 아래와 같다

1. 주한 미군을 고객으로 하는 접객 업소의

~9~

61

· 서-비스 개선

· 버의 시설 개선

· 위생 감독

2. 성명보균자 및 업태부의 선도

3. 마약의 소지 및 판매 단속

4. 미군표 거래 밀수 및 미군수물자의 암거래 단속

5. 주한 미군기관에 종사하는 한국 고용인과의 노사 분규

6. 기타 상호간의 권익의 침해 및 친선의 저해

제 4 조 (구성 및 위원의 위촉) ① 협의회의 한국측 구성원은 위원장 1인과 위원 5 내지 7인 및 간사 1인으로 구성한다

② 위원장은 시장이되고 위원은 위원장이 다음 기관의 대표 또는 구성원중에서 위촉하고 간사는 소속 공무원중에서 임명한다

62

1. 사법기관 (경찰 경찰 및 세관)

2. 노동행정 기관

3. 보건 위생 기관

4. 시정 자문위원회 또는 개발위원회

5. 정보기관

6. 관광업체 유흥및 요식업협회

7. 업태부 조합 (협회)

8. 기타 유관 기관 또는 시민 대표

③ 위원장은 위원중 다음 사유가 발생하였을 때
는 그 직을 사임게 하고 즉시 후임자를 선임 하
여야 한다

1. 본인이 사임코자 원할 때

2. 타 기관으로 전출 되었을 때

3. 회의 참여이 미온적이고 협의회 운영이 소극적
  일 때

4. 한미 친선을 해치는 행위를 하였거나 그려한

63

행위가 있다고 인정될 때

5. 기타 위원장이 필요하다고 인정될 때

제 5 조 (위원장 등의 직무) ① 위원장은 협의회를 대표

하고 회의의 의장이 된다

다만 위원장이 사고가 있을 때에는 위원중에서

위원장이 지정한 자가 그 직무를 대행한다

② 위원은 위원장의 명을 받아 협의회에 출석하

여 발언하며 부의된 안건을 상호 합의하고 토의한다

③ 간사는 위원장의 명을 받아 협의회에 출석하되

발언할 수 있으며 협의회의 서무를 처리 한다

제 6 조 (분임협의회) ① 협의회의 효율적 운영과 부의될

사항을 원활이 처리하기 위하여 협의회의 협의

를 거쳐 분임협의회를 구성할 수 있다 ② 분임

협의회의 위원은 위원장이 지명하고 위원의 수

는 2 내지 3 인으로 한다

③분임 협의회는 수임받은 사안이 완결되었을 때 자동적으로 해체된다

제 7 조 (회의) 협의회는 매월 1회 정기적으로 개최하되 개최일은 양측의 협의로 정하며 회의는 원활한 의사 교환을 도모하기 위하여 비공식적이어야 한다

다만 어느 일방의 요구가 있을 때는 수시 개최할 수 있다

제 8 조 (회의주관) ① 정기회는 상호 교대로 타방 위원을 초청하여 개최하되 초청한 기관이 주관한다

다만 전조 단서의 경우에는 요구기관에서 주관함을 원칙으로 한다

② 주관기관은 늦어도 회의 개최 5일전에 타방 대표에게 아래 사항이 기재된 내용을 서면으로 통지하여야 한다

1 회의 개최 일시

~23~

65

~24~

2. 회의 개최 장소

3. 부의안건 또는 개최코자 하는사유

4. 초청자와 피초청자의 기관및 대표명

③ 제6조의 규정에 의한 분임협의회는 양측의
사전협의를 거쳐 회의 일시와 장소를 따로히
정하머 개최할 수 있다

제9조 (협의회 해산) 주한 미군이 이동하거나 병영이
폐쇄되는 때는 자동적으로 해체된다

제10조 (참고인의 협의회출석) 협의회는 필요하다고 인
정할때에는 부의된 안건에 관련되는 관계인 또
는 참고인의 출석 발언이나 참고 자료의 제시
를 요청할 수 있다

제11조 (미결사안의 처리) 협의회에서 합의되지 못한
사안은 한미 합동위원회에서 건의 한다

제12조 (보고) ① 위원장은 아래 각호에 대하여 내무
부장관에게 보고한다

1 협의회 개최 상황

2. 제9조에 의한 협의회 해산 사항

3. 주한 미군과 지역 사회간의 불상사나 양측의
친선을 저해하는 문제의 발생또는 발생의 우려가 있는 사항

4 기타 중앙부처의 지원 또는 조정이 필요하거나 참고될 사항

② 제1항 제1호의 보고는 전월분을 익월 10일 까지

제2호와 제4호의 보고는 즉시 각각 서면 보고

하고 제3호의 보고는 지휘 보고로 한다

제13조 (기타사항) 협의회 운영에 필요한 다른 사항
은 협의회의 협의를 거쳐 따로히 정한다

부 칙

① (공포일) 이 조례는 공포한 날로 부터 시행한다

② (기준 위원회 폐지) 이 조례공포 당시에 설치되어 있는
기준의 각종 한미친선 조직은 본 조례에 의하여 구성되는
위원회에 폐지 통합한다

~25~

-61

PUSAN MUNICIPAL GOVERNMENT

REGULATION

NUMBER 707   26 July 1973.

ESTABLISHMENT OF PUSAN KOREAN -AMERICAN FRIENDSHIP COUNCIL

Proclaimed herewith is the regulation on establishment of the Pusan Korean - American Friendship
Council approved by minister of the Inferion Affairs Ministry. reference Ltr. Management 723 -1081
dated 22 June 1973.

                              Mayor Park Yung - su.
                              City of Pusan

Article 1 PURPOSE The purpose of this regulation is to stipulate the establishment and operation of the pusan Korean - American Friendship
Council (KAFC).

Article 2. ESTABLISHMENT OF KAFC. The KAFC

—27—

will be setablished for the purpose of insuring mutual Cooperation and ties through promotion of under-standing and goodwill between the US Armed Forces and the local community.

Article 3. <u>FUNCTIONS</u>.

(1) The KAFC will take appropriated and coordinated actions to resolve the items of mutual concern and also the potential or actual problems involving both parties by agreement thro-ugh mutual understanding and cooperation.

(2) The items of mutual concern are as follows:

1. Actions to improve business establishments catering to the US Armed Forces personnel;

    a. Improvement of services

    b. Improvement of interior and exterior facilites.

    c. Sanitary supervision.

2. Provision of proper guidance in the interest of business girls and VD carriers.

69

3. Cracking down on illegal possession and transaction of the narcotics.

4. Cracking down on illegal transaction of the military currency and black marketing of the US military spplies.

5. Labor - Management dipute involving the Korean national employees of the US Forces in Korea.

6. Infringement of the other party's prestige and obstruction of mutual friendship.

Article 4 <u>COMPOSITION.</u>

(1) The ROK KAFC component will be one Chairman, five fo seven members and one general/secretary.

(2) Mayor will serve as the chairman who will appoint the general/secretary. Each representative or a member of the following organizations will be commissioned to serve as KAFC members.

— 29 —

110

1. Law Enforcement (Prosecutors, Police and Custom Agents)

2. Labor Administration

3. Health and Sanitation

4. Advisory or Development Council for city Administration

5. Public Information Media

6. Tourism and Business Establishments Associations

7. Business Girls Unions

8. Other Related Activities or Citizens Representative

(3) The chairman will have a member resign from KAFC duties in case he is involved in the following situations.

1. When a member desires to resign from KAFC duties.

2. When a member is assigned to other activities

3. When a member is not interested in KAFC

activities with poor KAFC attendance record.

4. When there is a confirmed evidence that a
member obstructed mutual friendship.

5. When the chairman considers that a member's
continued KAFC service is not required.

Article 5. DUTIES OF CHAIRMAN AND MEMBERS.

(1) The chairman will erpresent the KAFC
and preside the meeting. In case the chairman is
unable to attend the meeting due to an incident,
one of the KAFC members will be designated by
the chairman to serve as the acting chairman.

(2) The KAFC members will be directed by the
chairman to attend council meetings and participate
in discussions on the matters referred to the council

(3) The general / secretary will also be directed by the chairman to attend council meetings
to attend to KAFC administrative duties. He has
however no voice in council discussions.

Article 6. SUBCOMMITTEES.

~ 31 ~

—32—

(1) Subcommittees may be established by agreement to deal with particular areas of interest to the council and to ensure effective council operation.

(2) The number of the subcommittee members will be two to three persons to be named by the chairman.

(3) The subcommittees will be automatically dissolved upon resolution or completion of the matters brought to council attention.

Article 7 <u>KAKC MEETINGS</u>. Council meetings will be scheduled each month with the date to be determined by agreement. However additional meetings may be scheduled at the request of one party. Council meetings will be proceeded in an informal manner conductive to the free and friendly interchange of opinions.

Article 8. HOST.

(1) Both components will alternate as host with the place of the meeting rotated accordingly. The additional meetings, reference Article 7 above, will be hosted basically by the party who requested the meeting.

(2) The hosting party will inform the other party of the following items in writing at least five days prior to the meeting.

1. Date of meeting

2. Place of meeting

3. Agenda or the reason for convening a meeting

4. List of attendees (name and assignment) of both the hosting and invited parties.

(3) Date and place of the subcommittee meetings, reference Article 6 above, may be determined by the committee by agreement.

Article 9. DISSOLUTION OF KAFC. The KAFC will

— 33 —

be automatically dissolved in case the camp/compound be closed or redeployed.

Article 10. <u>PRESENTATION OF WITNESSES.</u> When necessary the council may request witnesses or related personnel to be present at council meetings to speak or produce reference materials in support of the particular items of concern to the council.

Article 11. <u>UNRESOVED COUNCIL MATTERS.</u> Matters which cannot be resolved will be referred to ROKUS joint committee.

Article 12. <u>REPORTS.</u>

(1) The chairman will submit reports concerning the following items to minister of the Inferior Affairs Ministry:

1. KAFC meetings

2. Dissolution of KAFC. Article 9

3. Undesirable incidents involving US armed

Forces personnel and local community or actual or potential matters which may harm mutual friendship.

4. Other reference matters requiring support or intervention of the central government.

(2) The reports on par (1) - above be forwarded no later than the 10th day following the end of the month. However, the reports on par (1) - 2 and (1) - 4 above will be forwarded in writing immediately when the situation arises. The reports on par (1) - 3 should be made verbally.

Article 13. OTHER ITEMS. Any other items in support of the effective operation of KAFC may be stipulated by agreement.

SUPPLEMENT TO ABOVE REGULLTION

(1) Proclamation of KAFC Regulation: This regulation will be put into effect from the day it is

~ 35 ~

snb

proclaimed.

(2) Disolution of Existing Council : Existing council will be dissolved for its consolidation in the new KAFC organization.

Translated by : Mr. Yoo, Civil Affairs

기 안 용 지

분류기호 문서번호	미이 723 -	(전화번호)	전결규정 5 조 항 차관 전 결 사 항
처 리 기 간			
시 행 일 자	74. 7. 16.		*(서명)*
보 존 년 한			차 관

보조 기관	차 관 보	*(서명)*		협 조	기획관리실장	*(서명)*
	국 장	*(서명)*			총무과장	*(서명)*
	과 장	*(서명)*				
기 안 책 임 자	양 체 훈	북미 2 과				

경 유		발		통	
수 신	내 부 결 재				
참 조		신		제	

제 목	SOFA 군민관계 임시분과위원회의 미군 기지 현지 답사

1. 71. 9. 2. SOFA 군민관계임시분과위원회의 설립 이후 동

임시분과위원회는 지금 까지 26회에 걸친 주한미군 기지 및 주변 기지촌에

대한 한.미 합동 현지 답사를 실시하여, 미군 주둔에 따른 제반 문제 해결을

통한 주둔 조건의 향상 및 한미군민관계 개선에 기여하여 왔읍니다.

2. 상기 임시분과위원회는 74. 5. 3. 제27차 회의에서 합의

(별첨 회의록 참조)한바에 따라, 다음과 같이 미군 기지에 대한 현지 답사를

실시코저 하오니 이를 재가하여 주시기 바랍니다.

- 다 음 -

가. 현지답사 지역 :

  (1) 춘천지역 소재 미군 기지

  (2) 대구 지역 소재 미군 기지

나. 목　적 :

    (1)　미군기지 시찰 및 미군측 현황 청취

    (2)　기지촌 지역 지방관서의 현황 청취

    (3)　한미 공동 토의 및 문제점 해결 방안 강구

다. 여행 계획 :

    (1)　아측 참가자 :　군민관계 임시분과위원회

                           한국측 위원 12명

        의 장 :　외무부 북미2과장 서기관 이 상 훈

        간 사 :　외무부 북미2과 서기관 양 세 흠

        위 원 :　내무부 관리과장 서기관 전 병 우

                 치안국 외사과 총경 이 병 모

                 치안국 수사지도과 총경 유 명 두

                 법무부 법무실 검사 홍 유 택

                 법무부 검찰과 검사 신 창 언

                 교통부 관광진흥과장 서기관 감 철 용

                 보사부 만성병과장 서기관 오 영 일

                 보사부 마약과장 서기관 이 희 찬

                 문공부 외보과장 서기관 김 광 식

                 국방부 민사과장 대령 심 용 순

    (2)　여행 기간 :

        (가) 춘천지역 : 74. 8. 2. - 3.

        (나) 대구지역 : 74. 8. 22. - 24.

    (3)　이용편

        (가) 춘천지역 : 버스 왕복

(나) 대구지역: 항공 왕복

(4) 경비 지출 근거: 일반외교비 국내여비(SOFA 운영)

첨부: 동 회의록 1부.   끝.

0201—1—43A (2—2)
1972. 12. 29 승인

190mm×268mm(2급인쇄용지 60g/m²)
조 달 청 (2,000,000매 인쇄)

CITY OF CHINHAE

19 June 1974

Proposed city tour for AD HOC Sub-Committee on Civil - Military Relations

DTG	EVENT	REMARKS
1345	Depart U.S. Naval Facility	
1345 - 1355 (10)	Visit ROK Naval Base Command	
1400 - 1415 (15)	Visit ROK Naval Academy	
1425 - 1440 (15)	Tower	
1445 - 1450 (5)	Tour of Soy bean oil factory	
1455 - 1500 (5)	Tour of Hankuk plastic factory	
1505 - 1535 (30)	Tour of Chinhae fertilizer factory	
1540 - 1545 (5)	Tour of Ammo pier	
1600	Depart Chinhae airport	

I. Sick Calls - Medical/Dental Departments held COMREL/
    Sick Calls as follows:

    (July 1973 - May 1974)

A. Medical Sick Calls:

    (1) Bo Yuk Won   39 times   716 Patients
    (2) Deaf & Dumb Home   1 time   14 Patients
    (3) Dispensary   ----------   2,976 Patients
    (4) Referals to other   31 times   31 Patients
        Hospitals
                          TOTAL...................3,737 Patients

B. Dental Sick Calls:

    (1) Heang Am Dong   1 time   29 Patients
    (2) Bo Yuk Won   1 time   89 Patients
    (3) Ung Chon Dong   14 times   816 Patients
    (4) Koji Do Area   41 times   2,957 Patients
    (5) Dispensary   ----------   200 Patients

                      TOTAL...................4,089 Patients

                    G/TOTAL...................7,826 Patients

II. HANDCLASP - The COMREL Officer makes numerous visits
to the following institutions to distribute various items
from HANDCLASP:

A. Bo Yuk Won Orphanage, Chinhae

        (1) 64 Boxes - Assorted Food
        (2) 16 Boxes - Used Clothing
        (3) 18 Gallons - Fresh Milk
        (4) 1 Each - Sewing Machine
        (5) 1 Each - New Bath House
        (6) 1 Each - Cooking Pot
        (7) 24 Each - Baby Cribs
        (8) 7 Boxes - Toys
        (9) 64Each - Korean Bibles
        (10) 64 Each - Korean Hymnals
        (11) 13 Sets - School Uniforms

B. Hi Hang Won Orphanage, Chinhae

        (1) 29 Boxes - Assorted Food
        (2) 5 Boxes - Used Clothing
        (3) 12 Gallons - Fresh Milk

C. So Mang Won Orphanage, Chinhae

    (1) 27 Boxes - Assorted Food
    (2) 3 Boxes - Used Clothing
    (3) 12 Each (Gallons) Fresh Milk

D. (1) 30 Boxes - Assorted Food
    (2) 3 Boxes - Used Clothing
    (3) 12 Gallons Fresh Milk
    (4) 8 D/M Diesel Fuel

E. Sin Ai Won Orphanage, Chinhae

    (1) 45 Boxes - Assorted Food
    (2) 8 Boxes - Used Clothing
    (3) 1 Each - Sewing Machine

F. Kwang Won, Koje Do

    (1) 56 Boxes - Assorted Food
    (2) 2 Boxes - Used Clothing
    (3)

G. Orphanages, Masan (Through USA 609th Ordnance Depot)

    (4) 51 Boxes - Assorted Food

H. Old Ladies Home, Masan

    (1) 12 Bundles - Used Magazines

I. Public Schools in Chinhae and Masan

    (1) 60 Each - Basket Balls, etc.
    (2) 3 Each - World Atless

J. Hospitals:

    (1) Koje Do Clinic (Sil Chon Ri)
        (a) 56 Boxes - Assorted Medical Supplies
        (b) 1 Each - Boat Engine

    (2) Koje Christian Hospital (Chang Sang Do)
        (a) 57 Boxes - Assorted Medical Supplies

    (3) Masan National T.B. Hospital
        (a) 3 Boxes - Toys

    (4) International Christian Hospital, Ha Dong
        (a) 67 Boxes - Assorted Medical Supplies

2

83

III. CNFK COMREL PROJECTS

A. Playground equipment of swing/slide sets

    (1) Chinhae City area   - 2 sets
    (2) Koje Do area   - 1 set
    (3) Masan City area   - 1 set

B. A part of construction material for Chinhae reconstruction night school - W200,000

C. Medicines for destitute people :

    (1) Chinhae   W220,000
    (2) Kojo Do Is   200,000
                W420,000

D. A simple pipe water system for Tae Baek Dong, Chinhae W160,000

IV. Women's Welfare Committee Program

A. Milk and cookie party for Bo Yuk Won Orphange - once a month.

B. Chu Sok (Korean Thanksgiving day) Project for 50 destitute families - food stuffs and clothing.

C. Scholarship Program

    (1) 2 students at Beauty School - 6 mos course
    (2) 37 students at Radio School - 4 mos course
    (3) 38 students at Typing School - 3 mos course
    (4) 1 student at Boys' Sr Hi School - 3 yr course
    (5) 1 student at Bible College Taegu - 2 yr course
    (6) 1 student at Girls' Sr Hi School - 2 yr course

D. Emergency Medical Fund:

    (1) W272,000 worth of T.B. medication was purchased at local drug store for destitute patients seen by our medical officer.

    (2) W13,500 paid out for a needy patient on hospital bill.

V. "HELPING HAND" Project

A. 4 enlisted men of CF-USNFK helped paint 2 baby rooms of Bo Yuk Won orphanage.

B. 9 ladies of CF-USNFK helped paint a chapel of Bo Yuk Won.

C. 8 ladies of CF-USNFK helped paint a building of Sin Ai Won, Yng Chon.

D. 20 men from USS GURKE (DD 783) helped paint 9 childrens rooms plus a dining hall at Bo Yuk Won.

E. 25 men from USS COOK (DE 1083) helped paint 7 childrens rooms plus their library room.

F. USS WORDEN (DLG 18) provided refreshments for childrens party at Bo Yuk Won. The combo bank also provided music.

VI. A water pump was loaned out to Chinhae City to assit getting water to dried rice paddies in area during long drought on 13 JUL 73.

VII. 23 children of C. Turner Joy Elementary School, CF-USNFK, participated in the program of "International Friendship Childrens Night" which was held 19 APR 74 at Chinhae Theater during the 12th Harbor (Cheery Blossom) Festival.

VIII. Chinhae City Korean-American Friendship Council – 2 meetings were held.

소양강다목적댐 및 수력발전소

SOYANG-GANG MULTI-PURPOSE DAM AND HYDRO POWER PLANT

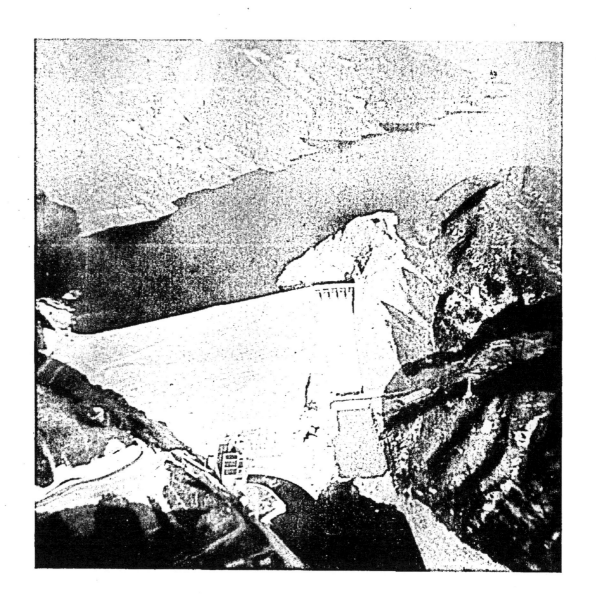

산 업 기 지 개 발 공 사
Industrial Sites & Water Resources Development Corp.(ISWACO)

소 양 강 다 목 적 댐 관 리 사 무 소
Soyang-Gang Multi-Purpose Dam Office

'86

3. 시설현황 (Out-line of Facilities)

댐 Dam

형식 (Type)	전토 심벽 사녀댐 Zone-Fill Dam of Central Coretype
높이 (Height)	123m
길이 (Length)	530m
넓이 (Bottom width)	550m
체적 (Embankment Volume)	9,591,200㎥

저수지 Reservoir

계획홍수위 (Design Flood Water Surface)	EL. 198
상시만수위 (Normal High Water Surface)	EL. 193.50
이용수심 (Draw Down)	48m
유역면적 (Catchment Area)	2,703㎢
저수용량 (Storage Capacity)	29억톤 2.9 Billion Ton
유효저수량 (Efective Capacity)	21억톤 2.1 Billion Ton
만수면적 (Reservoir Area)	70㎢

여수로 Spill Way

형식 (Type)	슈트식 여수로 Open chute Spill Way
수문 (Gate)	Tainter Gate 13m×13m×5 Gates
일류부표고 (Over Flow Crest Elevation)	EL. 185.50

수로 Water Way

취수구 (Intake)	Bellmouthed Type W=10m L=25m H=20m×2Line
취수탑 (Intake Tower)	D=10m H=64.5m
터널 (Tunnel)	D=8.5m~9.0m L=708m
조압수조 (Surge Tank)	Chamber Type
수압철관로 (Penstock)	7m⌀×87.5m×1 Line 4.95~4.5m⌀×101m×2 Line

관계용수설비 Irrigation Facilities

수압철관로 (Penstock Line)	2m⌀×84.6m×1 Line
방수용량 (Discharge capacity)	Hollow Jet valve 50㎥/s×1 Unit 1㎥/s×1 Unit

수차 Water Turbine

형식 (Type)	입축 후랑시스형 Vertical Francis Type
용량 (Capacity)	103,000kw
대수 (Number of unit)	2 Sets
회전수 (Speed)	180 r.p.m.
사용수량 (Turbine Discharge)	최대시 (max) : 250㎥/Sec.
유효낙차 (Efective Head)	최대시 (max) : 110m 최소시 (min) : 66.5m

발전기 Generator

형식 (Type)	입축 우산형 3상교류동기 발전기 3-Phase Vertical Umbrella Type
용량 (Capacity)	110,000 KVA
대수 (Number of unit)	2 Sets
발전전력 (Plant Out-Put)	최대출력 200,000 KW
년간발전량 (Annual Energy Out Put)	353,000,000KWH

1. Out-line of the Project

This multi-purpose dam project is planned as a part of the integrated development plan for Han River basin with the object of advanced control of natural river run off by the construction of a zonefill dam across a narrow valley in the Soyang River. The dam is located 12 kilometers from the confluence of the Soyang River and the North Han River, and 13 kilometers northeast from Chunchon city.

The development of the potential water resources at this dam site will generate a substantial amount of electric power, provide municipal, industrial, and irrigation water supples, and also significantly reduce flood damages in downstream reaches, especially in the Seoul and Kyung-In district. Annual energy production will be...353,000,000 Kwh. with an installed capacity of 200,000 Kw. This power will assist greatly in meeting the rapidly increasing power loads that accompany the booming economic development of the Republic.

The firm water supplies made available will be essential to the increase of power generation at downstream power plants, agricultural production, the growth of industry and the rise in living standards.

This dam construction project was started on April 15, 1967 and completed on October 15, 1973 and total construction cost of the project is 27.4 billion wons. The total number of persons, heavy equipment and materials required for the project were 6,170,000 mandays, 540,000 car-days, 2,167,000 bags of cement and 15,000 tons of iron and steel respectively.

1. 사업의 개요

본 다목적댐은 춘천시 동북방 13km 북한강 지류인 소양강 상류에 자연유량(自然流量)을 고도로 조절할 목적으로 협착(俠窄)하는 한강수계 중항계반에 사력(砂礫)댐을 축조하는 다목적 사업이다. 이 댐은 소양강과 북한강 본류의 합류점에서 12km 지점에 위치하며 보다 유효한 수자원 개발로서 이 댐지점의 한강하류연안의 수도 서울 및 경인 지역의 막대한 홍수피해의 방지와 급격하게 경제성장하는 수반되어 전력수요를 위한 시설용으로 전원개발의 필요성에 부응하는 시설로서 연평균 353,000,000kwh를 생산 공급하는 동시에 하류지역의 발전전력을 증가하고 또한 하천유수의 발전(發電)에 따르는 도시 공업용수와 계절용수 공급등을 목적으로 하는 다목적 대규모 수자원 개발 사업이다. 이 댐은 1967. 4. 15 착공하여 1973. 10. 15 완공된 것으로 총 공사비 270여억원이 투입되었습니다. 공사에 동원된 인원은 6,170,000명, 보한 연 540,000 대의 중장비 2,167,000대의 시멘트 그리고 15,000 T의 철강재가 사용되었습니다.

2. 사업효과 (Effects of the Project)

홍수조절용량 (Exclusive Flood Control Space)	500×10⁶㎥
용수공급 (Water Supply)	1,213×10⁶㎥/yr
평균발전량 (Annual Energy output)	353×10⁶kwh/yr.
하류발전량증가 (Increased Energy output in Downstream Power Stations)	61×10⁶kwh/yr.

4. 댐 단면도 (Typical Section of Dam)

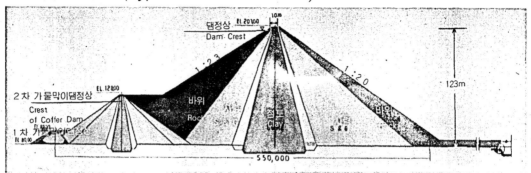

5. 수로 단면도 (Typical Section of waterway)

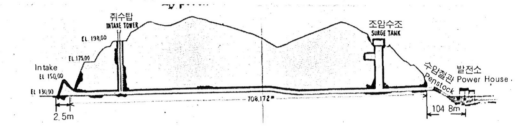

6. 댐 부근 평면도 (General Layout of Dam Area)

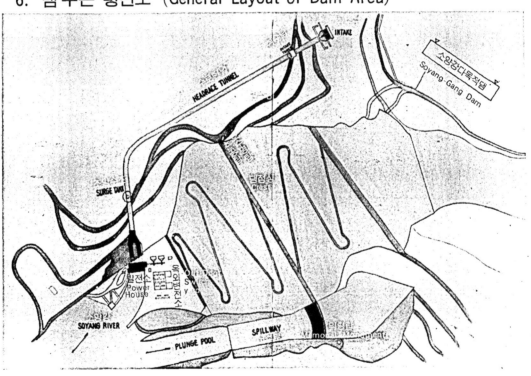

SCHEDULE FOR TRIP
AD HOC SUBCOMMITTEE ON CIVIL-MILITARY RELATIONS
TRIP TO CHUNCHON - CAMP PAGE

Friday, 23 August 1974

0830	Bus Departs Yongsan with US Component - From Bldg. 2370
0845	Bus Departs ROK Capitol Building with ROK Component
1115	Scheduled Arrival at Camp Page
1130	Luncheon for Ad Hoc Subcommittee at Camp Page
1300	Welcome by the Commander of the US Army Fourth Missile Command and Briefings by US Officials
1400	Presentations by Korean Officials at Office of Mayor of Chunchon
1500	Visit to Soyang Dam and other points of interest
1800	Dinner hosted by Korean Officials
1900	Visit Clubs in Chunchon (map attached)
2000	Depart for Seoul
2230	Arrive Back in Seoul

INCLOSURE 1

89

MAP OF DOWNTOWN CHUNCHON

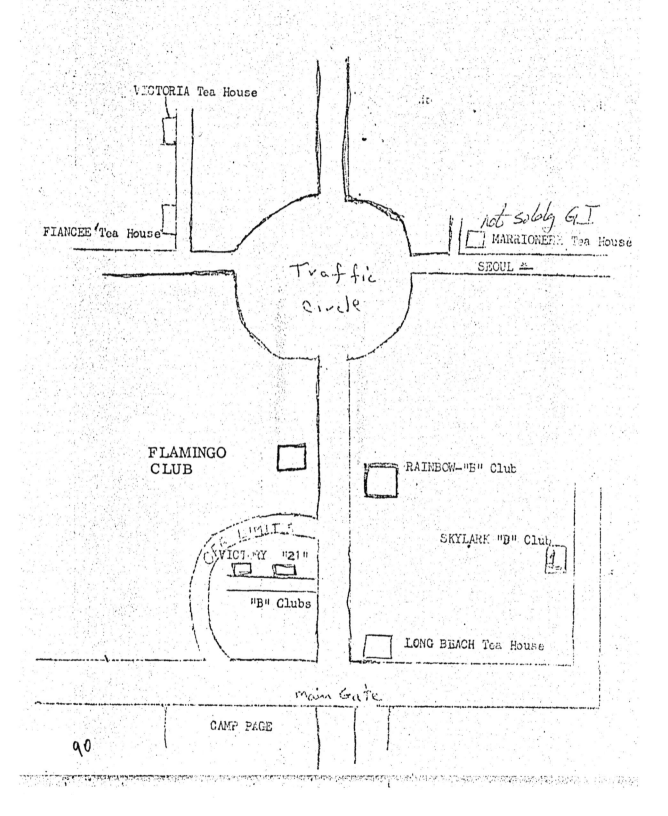

PARTICIPANTS IN TRIP OF US-ROK AD HOC SUBCOMMITTEE ON
CIVIL-MILITARY RELATIONS TO CHUNCHON - 23 AUGUST 1974

ROK COMPONENT

Mr. LEE Sang Hoon
Chief, North America Division II
Ministry of Foreign Affairs

Mr. YANG Sei Hoon
North America Division II
Ministry of Foreign Affairs

Mr. JEON Byoung Woo
Chief, Management Section
Ministry of Home Affairs

Mr. HONG Yu Taek
Prosecutor, Claims Section
Ministry of Justice

ROK COMPONENT

LTC AN Woo Il
Civil Affairs Division
Office of Emergency Planning Coordinator
Ministry of National Defense

Mr. KIM Chol Yong
Chief, Tourism Promotion Section
Ministry of Transportation

Mr. CHOI Jong Soo
Management Section
Ministry of Home Affairs

Mr. KIM Dong Jae
Narcotics Section
Ministry of Health and Social Affairs

US COMPONENT

CAPT W. E. Sharp, USN
Assistant Chief of Staff, J5

COL Gilbert Procter, Jr.
Deputy Chief of Staff, Army

COL William A. Zeigler
Judge Advocate, US Forces, Korea

LTC D. C. Warren
Surgeon's Office, US Forces, Korea

MAJ Thom O'Hara
Chief, Operations and Plans Div.
PMO

US COMPONENT

Mr. R. A. Kinney
Chief, International Relations Branch
J5 Division

MAJ W. E. Schmidt
International Relations Branch
J5 Division

Mr. AN Chang Hun
J5, Interpreter

Inclosure 2

91

공   란

공   란

공   란

공   란

공 란

공   란

기 안 용 지

분류기호 문서번호	미이 723	(전화번호)	전결규정 조 항	
			국장 전결사항	
처리기간				
시행일자	74. 8. 8.		국 장	
보존년한				
보조기관	과 장		협	
기안책임자	양세훈	북미 2과	조	
경유 수신 참조	수신처 참조			
제 목	SOFA 군민관계 임시 분과위원회의 기지촌 현지답사 실시.			

74. 5. 3. SOFA 군민관계 임시분과위원회 제 27차 회의에서

합의된 바에 따라, 다음과 같이 미군기지 및 주변기지촌에 대한 한미

합동 현지 답사를 실시할 예정이니 각 위원들은 필히 참석하여 주시기

바랍니다.

　　　　　　　　　- 다 　 음 -

1. 현지 답사 지역 : 대구 및 춘천지역 소재 미군기지

2. 목적 　　　 :

　　가. 미군기지 시찰 및 미국측 현황 파악.

　　나. 기지촌 지역 지방관서의 현황 파악.

　　다. 한미 공동 토의 및 문제점 해결 방안 강구.

3. 여행기간 :

　　가. 대구 지역 : 74. 8. 16 - 18

나. 춘천 지역 : 74. 8. 23 - 24

4. 참가자 : 군민관계 임시 분과위원희 위원

5. 경 비 : 외무부 부담.

6. 세부일정: 추후 통보.   끝.

수신처 : 내무부 장관 (관티 과장, 외사과장, 수사지도 과장)

　　　　법무부 장관 (송무 과장, 검찰각장)

　　　　교통부 장관 (관광국 진흥 과장)

　　　　보건사휙부 장관 (만성병과장, 마약과장)

　　　　문학공보부 장관 (해외공보 관 외보 과장)

　　　　국방부 장관 (비상계휙관실 민사정책담당관)

0201—1—43A (2—2)　　　　　　　　190m m×268m m (2 급인쇄용지 60g/m²)
1972. 12. 29 승인　　　　　　　　　조　달　청　(2,000,000매 인쇄)

기 지 촌 대 책 사 업 현 황

대 구 시

일 반 현 황

위 치

- 동경 — 128° 31′ ~ 41′
- 북위 — 35° 45′ ~ 57′
- 해발 — 40.69 ^{m}

면 적

- 행 정 구 역 — 178.32 ^{km}
- 그린벨트구역 — 531.02 〃
- 도시계획구역 — 735.9 〃

인구 및 가구

- 인구 — 1,200,273 명

  남 : 593,779 〃 (49 %)

  여 : 606,494 〃 (51 %)

- 가구 — 251,045 세대

기지촌 위치

- 켐프헨리 — 남구 대봉동
- 켐프워커 — 남구 대명동
- 켐프죠지 — 남구 봉덕동

-1-

10

기지촌대책사업현황

구 분	사 업 명	73		74		비 고
		계 획	실 적	계 획	진도	
친선활동						
	한 미 친 선 회 의	14 회	14 회	14 회	57 %	
	간 행 물 발 간	12 "	12 "	12 "	66 %	
환경정비						
	도 로 축 조	·	·	2 개소	30 %	잔여 2 개소
	·총계획 4 개소			L = 1,490		L = 985
	L = 2,475			미군지원장비		75 시 공
				연 264 대		
				(불도자외2종)		
	도 로 포 장	2 개소	2개소	1 개소	100 %	잔여 3.개소
	·총계획 6 개소	L = 2,120	L=	L = 855		L = 2,800
	L = 5,775		2,120			75 시 공
	인 도 포 장	·	·	2 개소		잔여 1 개소
	·총계획 3 개소			L = 1,600		L = 600
	L = 2,200					75 시 공

-2-

102

구 분	사 업 명	73		74		비 고
		계 획	실 적	계 획	진 도	
	하 수 도 개 수	1개소	1개소	4개소	90%	잔여 2개소
	• 총계획 7개소	L = 400	L = 400	L = 1,070		75 이후시공
	본관 L = 1,740					
	측구 L = 490					
	복개 L = 530					
	가 로 등 설 치	1개소	1개소	•	•	잔여 2개소
	• 총계획 3개소	23 등	23 등			70 등
	93 등					75 이후시공
	L = 2,800					
	가 로 수 식 재	•	•	2개소		
	• 총계획 2개소			520 본		
	프라타나스 520본					

-3-

구 분	사 업 명	73		74		비 고
		계 획	실 적	계 획	진 도	
보건대책						
	관광업소위생검사	23 회	43 회	106 회	70 %	
	마약및습관성위약품단속	30 ″	30 ″	8 ″	62 ″	
	결 핵 예 방	200 명	1,280 명	250 명	70 ″	
	성병진료소건립	2 층	2 층			1층:진료소
		90 명	90 명			2층:부 녀
						직업보도소
	성병예방및치료	12,488 명	28,400 명	1,570 명	120 ″	
	휴지통설치및도색	설 치	설치	도 색	100 ″	
		30 개소	30개소	30 개소		
사회대책						
	윤 락 여 성 선 도	4 회	32 회	24 회	62 %	
	담 화 문	1 ″	1 ″			
	직 업 보 도 및 훈 련	170 명	135 명	100 명	52 ″	
	어린이놀이터설치			대지 276 평	100 ″	기재미군지원
				그네외 4 종		
				5 대		

- 4 -

ㅣ마

공   란

공   란

공　　　란

공   란

공 란

공　　　　　란

Status of
U S Army Camp Area Improvement Projects

City of Daegu

Location:

East Longitude : 128°31′ ~ 128°41′

North Latitude : 35°45′ ~ 35°57′

Sea Level : 40.69 m

Area:

Administrative Area : 178.32 km^2

Greenbelt Area : 531.02 km^2

City Planning Area : 735.9 km^2

Population & Households :

Population : 1,200,273

male : 593,779 (49 %)

female : 606,494 (51 %)

Households : 251,045

Location of US Army Camps :

Camp Henry : Daebong Dong, NamKu

Camp Walker : Daemyong Dong, NamKu

Camp George : Bongduk Dong, NamKu

-1-

112

Camp Area Improvement Projects

Projects	Items	1973 Planned	1973 Completed	1974 Planned	1974 Progress (%)	Remarks
Friendship Activities	o KAFO Meeting	14	14	14	57	
	o Brochure	12	12	12	66	
Beautification of Camp Areas	o Construction of Roads · Total Planned 4 L = 2,475 m			2 projects L = 1,490 US Army Support w/ Heavy Equip. Total 264	30	2 projects to be carried over to 1975 L = 985
	o Road Pavement · Total Planned 6 L = 5,775 m	2pro. L = 2,120	2pro. L = 2,120	1pro. L = 855	100	3 projects to be carried over to 1975 L = 2,800
	o Pavement of Pedestrian Road. Total Planned 3 L = 2,200			2pro. L = 1,600		1 projects to be carried over to 1975 L = 600
	o Improvement of Drainage System Total : 7 projects · Main ditches L = 1,740	1pro. L = 400	1pro. L = 400	4pro. L = 1,070	90	2 projects to be carried over to 1975

- 2 -

Projects	Items	1973		1974		Remarks
		Planned	Completed	Planned	Progress (%)	
	· Side ditches L = 490					
	· Construction of Roads by covering ditches L = 530					
	o Installation of Street Lights · Total : 3 projects (93 Lights) L = 2,800	1 place 23 Lights	1 place 23 Lights			2 projects w/70 Lights to be started after 1975
	o Planting of trees along the streets · Total Planned 2 place 520 plane trees			2 pro. 520 trees		
Health & Sanitation Program	o Sanitary Inspection of Tourist Hotels	23	43	106	70	
	o Drug Insp.	30	30	8	62	
	o T.B. Insp.	200	1,280	250	70	

-3-

Projects	Items	1973		1974		Remarks
		Planned	Completed	Planned	Progress (%)	
	○ Const. of Health Center	2 story 90 pyong	2 story 90 pyong			1st story-Inspection Room 2nd story-Vocational Trng Room
	○ V.D. checks & Prevention	12,488	28,400	1,570	120	
	○ Wastecan & Painting	30	30	Painting 30	100	
Welfare Program	○ Guiding Prostitutes	4	32	24	62	
	○ Poster	1	1			
	○ Vocationat trng	170	135	100	52	
	○ Const. of Playground			276 pyong W/S equip.	100	Equipment provided by US Army

- 4 -

공   란

공 란

공   란

공　　　　　　란

공   란

공   란

기 안 용 지

분류기호 문서번호	미이 723 -	(전화번호)	전 결 규 정	조 항
			차 관	전 결 사 항

처 리 기 간		
시 행 일 자	1974. 9. 11.	
보 존 년 한		

보 조 기 관	차 관 보		협 조	기획관리실장
	국 장			총 무 과 장
	과 장			

| 기 안 책 임 자 | 유 광 석 | 북미 2과 | | |

경 수 참	유 신 조	건 의	발 신	통 제

제 목	SOFA 군민관계 임시분과위원회 미군 기지촌 현지 답사

1. 71. 9. 2. SOFA 군민관계 임시분과위원회의 설립 이후

동 위원회는 지금까지 27회에 걸친 주한미군 기지및 주변기지촌에 대한

한.미 합동 현지답사를 실시하여, 미군 주둔에 따른 제반문제 해결을

통한 미군 주둔조건의 향상및 한.미 군민관계 개선에 기여하여 왔읍니다.

2. 상기 임시분과위원회는 74. 5. 3. 제27차 회의에서 합의한바에

따라, 다음과 같이 미군기지에 대한 현지 답사를 실시코자 하오니 이를

재가하여 주시기 바랍니다.

- 다   음 -

가. 현지 답사 지역 : 군산, 동두천, 평택, 오산

나. 목   적 :

(1) 미군기지 시찰 및 미군측 현황 청취

	정 서
	관 인
	발 송

0201-1-8 A (갑)
1969. 11. 10 승 인   190㎜×268㎜ (특급인쇄용지 40g/㎡)
                                            조 달 청 (1,000,000매 인 쇄)

(2) 기지촌 지역 지방관서의 현황 청취

(3) 한.미 공동 토의 빛 분제점 해결방안 강구

다. 출장 계획 :

   (1) 아측 참가자 : 군민관계 임시분과위원회 위원 12명

      의   장 : 외무부 북미2과장 서기관 이상훈

      간   사 : 외무부 북미2과 서기관 양세훈 ✓

      위   원 : 내무부 관리과장 서기관 전병우

               치안국 외사관 총경 이병노

               치안국 수사지도과 총경 유병두

               법무부 법무실 검사 홍유택

               법무부 검찰과 검사 신창언

               교통부 관광진흥과장 서기관 김정용

               보사부 만성병과장 서기관 오영일

               보사부 마약과장 서기관 이희찬

               문공부 외보과장 서기관 김광식

               국방부 민사과장 대령 심용순

   (2) 출장기간 : (가) 평택, 오산 10. 11.

                 (나) 군산 10. 17 - 19

                 (다) 동두천 10. 25

   (3) 이용편 : 버스 왕복

   (4) 예산항목 : 일반외교비 국내여비 (SOFA 운영)

                        끝.

기 안 용 지

분류기호 문서번호	미이723-	(전화번호)	전결규정	조 항
			전결사항	
처리기간	**지 급**			
시행일자	1974.11.4.		국 장	
보존년한				
보조기관	과 장		협	
기안책임자	유광석 북미2과			
경유 수신 참조	수신처 참조			
제 목	군민관계 임시분과위원회 기지촌			

74.11.8.(금) 예정된 한미 주둔군 지위협정 군민관계 임시

분과위원회 제30차 회의대신 동일, 군산지역 기지촌을 별첨 일정에

따라 시찰하기로 계획이 변경되었으니 각 위원께서는 꼭히 참석

하여 주시기 바랍니다.

첨 부 : 시찰일정 1부. 끝.		정서
수신처 : 내무부장관 (관리과장, 외사과장, 수사지도과장)		
법무부장관 (송무과장, 검찰과장)		관인
보건사회부장관 (만성병과장, 마약과장)		
교통부장관 (관광진흥과장)		
문화공보부장관 (해외공보관 외보과장)		발송
국방부장관 (민사정책담당관)		

0201-1-8A (갑)
1969. 11. 10 승 인

190mm×268mm (특급인쇄용지 40g/m²)
조 달 청 (1,000,000매 인 쇄)

기상 서류나 대문에 연기함.

Ad Hoc Subcommittee on Civil-Military Relations

Proposed Itinerary for Trip to Kunsan - 8 November 1974

0900	Depart by Helicopter from H-201 (Yongsan Helipad)
1030	Arrive Kunsan Air Base - Bus to Briefing Room
1045/1200	Briefing at Kunsan Air Base
1200/1300	Lunch at Kunsan Air Base
1300/1400	Enroute to and Visit Silvertown
1400/1415	Bus to Kunsan City
1415/1530	Briefings and Tour at Kunsan City
1530	Bus to Kunsan Air Base
1600	Depart for Seoul
1730	Arrive at H-201 in Seoul

8 people maximum

125

기안용지

분류기호 문서번호	미 이723-	(전화번호 70-2324)	전결규정	조 항
			전결사항	

처리기간				
시행일자	1974.11.30.		국 장	*(서명)*
보존년한				

보 조 기 관	과 장	*(서명)*		협	
				조	

| 기안책임자 | 유광석 | 북미2과 | | |

경 유				
수 신	수신처 참조			
참 조				

제 목   SOFA 군민관계 임시분과위원회 기회론 변경검사.

74.5.3. 군민관계 임시분과위원회 제27차 회의시 합의한

바에따라, 군산지역 기지촌을 별첨 일정에따라 시찰하기로

결정되었으니, 각 위원께서는 참석 여부를 유선통보해 주시기

바랍니다.

첨 부 : 시찰일정 1부.   끝. | 정서 |

수신처 : 내무부장관 (관리과장, 외사과장, 수사지도과장)	
법무부장관 (송무과장, 검찰과장)	관인
보건사회부장관 (만성병과장, 마약과장)	
교통부장관 (관광진흥과장)	
문화공보부장관 (해외공보관 외보과장)	발송
국방부장관 (민사정책담당관)	

0201-1-8 A (갑)
1969. 11. 10 승인

190mm×268mm (특급인쇄용지 40g/m²)
조 달 청 (1,000,000매 인 쇄)

126

AD HOC SUBCOMMITTEE ON CIVIL - MILITARY RELATIONS

PROPOSED ITINERARY FOR TRIP TO KUNSAN - 10 DECEMBER 1974

0900	Depart by Helicopter from H-201 (Yongsan Helipad)
1030	Arrive Kunsan Air Base - Bus to Briefing Room
1045/1200	Briefing at Kunsan Air Base
1200/1230	Lunch at Kunsan Air Base
1230/1330	Enroute to and Visit Silvertown
1330/1345	Bus to Kunsan City
1345/1500	Briefings and Tour at Kunsan City
1500	Bus to Kunsan Air Base
1530	Depart for Seoul
1700	Arrive at H-201 in Seoul

AD HOC SUBCOMMITTEE ON CIVIL-MILITARY RELATIONS

PROPOSED ITINERARY FOR TRIP TO KUNSAN-10 DECEMBER 1974

0900	Depart by Helicopter from H-201 (Yongsan Helipad)
1030	Arrive Kunsan Air Base-Bus to Briefing Room
1045/1200	Briefing at Kunsan Air Base
1200/1230	Lunch at Kunsan Air Base
1230/1330	Enroute to and Visit Silvertown
1330/1345	Bus to Kunsan City
1335/1500	Briefing and Tour at Kunsan City
1500	Bus to Kunsan Air Base
1530	Depart for Seoul
1700	Arrive at H-201 in Seoul

128

외   무   부

미이 723-   1974. 12. 1.

수신 :

참조 :

제목 :   SOFA   군민관계 임시분과위원회 기지촌 현지 답사

  74. 5. 3. 군민관계 임시분과위원회 제27차 회의시 합의안
에 의거, 군산 지역 기지촌을 74. 12. 10. 별첨 일정에 따라 시찰
하기로 결정되었으니, 각 위원께서는 참석 여부를 우선 통보해주시기
바랍니다.

첨부 : 시찰 일정 1부.   끝.

외   무   부   장   관

기 안 용 지

분류기호 문서번호	미이 723 -		(전화번호 70-2324)	전결규정 조 항 국장 전결사항		
처리기간						
시행일자	1974. 12. 14.					
보존년한			국 장			

보조기관: 과 장

협조: 公文 대신
通報함.
12. 16.

기안책임자: 유 광 석   북미 2과

경유
수신
참조: 수신처 참조   발신   통제

제 목: SOFA 군민관계 임시분과위원회 기지촌 현지 답사

연 : 미이 723 - 50744 (74. 11. 30.)

미측 위원장의 견질로 인해 무기 연기되었던 연호 군산지역
기지촌 현지답사 일정이 별첨과 같이 12. 19.로 결정되었으니, 각
위원께서는 참석 여부를 12. 17.까지 유선 통보해주시기 바랍니다.

첨부 : 시찰 일정 1부.   끔.

수신처 : 내무부장관 (관리과장, 외사과장, 수사지도 과장)
법무부장관 (송무 과장, 검찰과장)
보건사회부장관 (만성병과장, 마약과장)
고통부장관 (관광진흥 과장)
문화공보부장관 (해외공보관 외보 과장)
국방부장관 (민사정책담당관)

정서

관인

발송

0201-1-8A (갑)
1969. 11. 10 승인

190mm×268mm (2급인쇄용지60g/m²)
조 달 청 (1,000,000매 인 쇄)

AD HOC SUBCOMMITTEE ON CIVIL-MILITARY RELATIONS

PROPOSED ITINERARY FOR TRIP TO KUNSAN-19 DECEMBER 1974

0840   용산 우체국앞

0900   Depart by Helicopter from H-201 (Yongsan Helipad)

1030   Arrive Kunsan Air Base - Bus to Briefing Room

1045/1200   Briefing at Kunsan Air Base

1200/1230   Lunch at Kunsan Air Base

1230/1330   Enroute to and Visit Silvertown

1330/1345   Bus to Kunsan City

1345/1500   Briefings and Tour at Kunsan City

1500   Bus to Kunsan Air Base

1530   Depart for Seoul

1700   Arrive at H-201 in Seoul

131

공 란

공   란

공   란

공   란

공　　란

공   란

공   란

공   란

공　　　란

공 란

공 란

SUBCOMMITTEE MEMBERS PARTICIPATING IN KUNSAN VISIT
19 December 1974

US Component

Colonel Gilbert Procter, Jr., USA (DCS Army)
* Captain David G. Ramsey, USN (J5)
Major Walter E. Schmidt, USAF (J5)
Mr. AN Chang Hun, KNCIV (J5)
Major Thomas C. O'Hara, USA (PMJ)
Colonel Louis E. Herrick, USAF (J1)
Major Ferd W. McEntire, USA (Surgeon)
Lt Colonel David W. Lacy, USA (J5)
Mr. John Boardman, USCIV (AMEMB)

ROK Component

KIM Chol Yong (MOT)
HONG Yu Taek (MOJ)
SHIN Yong Yul (KNP)
HWANG Min Taik (MOHA)
* YANG Sei Hoon (MOFA)
OH Jung Il (MOFA)
LEW Kwang Suck (MOFA)

* INDICATES CHAIRMEN

143

Incl 2

LOCAL KUNSAN OFFICIALS WHO TOOK PART IN THE BASE/CITY BRIEFINGS

City Mayor	CHAE Bong Chae
Vice Mayor	CHUNG Jae Bong
Judge	KO A Do
Chief Police Superintendent	BAEK Chung Ki
Fire Marshal Superintendent	KANG Duck Hyung
CO, ROKA Security Command Detachment	Major NAM Kwan Hee
President, Chung Ku Lumber Company	PAK Hee Bong
City PIO	YI Yong Kon
OKKU KUN Chief	KONG Chung Oh

Incl 3

OFF-BASE OFFENSES IN THE KUNSAN AREA
January - November 1974

Monthly Totals

January	9
February	5
March	3
April	3
May	5
June	18
July	3
August	6
September	11
October	8
November	4
	75

Itemized Breakdown

Traffic Accident	23
Marijuana	10
Assault	28
Destruction of Private Properties	9
Theft of Private Properties	1
Failure to Pay Just Debt	2
Black Marketing	2
	75

Case Where ROKG Assumed Jurisdiction

Date of incident: 14 August 1972
Date ROKG assumed jurisdiction: 28 August 1972
Date trial concluded: 11 May 1973
Trial Court: Chonchu District Court
Name of Accused: Sgt Ortney L. Strickland
413-82-4011
8 FMS
Charge: Interference with official duty of KNP in uniform
Sentence: 10 months imprisonment suspended for 2 years

Incl 4

145

J-5 Memorandum

12 December 1974

To: US Component
Ad Hoc Subcommittee on Civil-Military
Relations

SUBJECT: Trip to Kunsan

Attached herewith is the itinerary for the trip to
Kunsan by the Ad Hoc Subcommittee on Civil-Military
Relations. This trip is scheduled for Thursday, 19
December 1974. The same approximate itinerary
is being followed as was previously scheduled but
had to be cancelled. Details about the Kunsan area
are also attached.

PAUL V. COLAIANNI
LTC, USAF
ACofS, J5

2 Incl

AD HOC SUBCOMMITTEE ON CIVIL - MILITARY RELATIONS

PROPOSED ITINERARY FOR TRIP TO KUNSAN - 19 DECEMBER 1974

0900	Depart by Helicopter from H-201 (Yongsan Helipad)
1030	Arrive Kunsan Air Base - Bus to Briefing Room
1045/1200	Briefing at Kunsan Air Base
1200/1230	Lunch at Kunsan Air Base
1230/1330	Enroute to and Visit Silvertown
1330/1345	Bus to Kunsan City
1345/1500	Briefings and Tour at Kunsan City
1500	Bus to Kunsan Air Base
1530	Depart for Seoul
1700	Arrive at H-201 in Seoul

공 란

공   란

화일번호 08

0001

정/리/보/존/문/서/목/록

기록물종류	문서-일반공문서철	등록번호	26021 9417	등록일자	2006-06-21
분류번호	729.419	국가코드		주제	

문서철명   SOFA 한.미국 합동위원회 군민관계 임시분과위원회 - 주한 미국 군인 기지촌 현지답사, 1976

생산과	북미2과	생산년도	1976 - 1976	보존기간	영구
담당과(그룹)	미주	안보		서가번호	--

창조분류

권차영

내용목차

마/이/크/로/필/름/사/항

촬영연도	*름 번호	화일 번호	후레임 번호	보관함 번호
2006-11-29	G-06-0046	08	1-55	

0002

기 안 용 지

분류기호 문서번호	디이763 -	(전화번호 70-2324)	전결규정 조 합 국 장 전 결 사 항
처 리 기 간		국 장	
시 행 일 자	1976. 4. 27.		
보 존 년 한			
보조기관	심 의 관		협
	과 장		
기안책임자	이 장 호	북미2과	
경 유			발 송
수 신	수신처 참조		1976. 4. 30. 외무부
참 조			
제 목	SOFA 군민관계 임시분과위원회 기지촌 시찰		

4. 8. 개최된 제33차 SOFA 군민관계 임시분과위원회에서
토의(별첨 참조)된 바 있는 미군 기지촌 시찰 계획이 다음과 같이
확정되었으니 동 시찰 참여 여부를 5. 3. 까지 필히 통보하여 주시기
바랍니다.

- 다 음 -

1. 시찰 장소

   포천군 동두천읍 소재 Camp Casey 및 동 주변 기지촌

2. 시찰 일자

   1976년 5월 12일 (수)

   (당일 출발하여 당일 귀경 계획이며 출발 시간 및 장소는

   추후 통보)

3. 참 여 자

   한.미 군민관계 임시분과위원회 한.미 위원 전원

0201-1-8A (강)
1969. 11. 10 승인
190mm×268mm (2급인쇄용지60g/m²)
조 달 청 (1,500,000매 인 쇄)

참부 : 제 33차 임시분과의원회의록 사본 1부, 끝

수신처 : 내무부장관 (지방국 도시지도 과장,

           치안본부 외사과장,

           치안본부 수사지도 과장)

       법무부장관 (법무실 송무과장, 검찰국 검찰 1 과장)

       국방부장관 (동원예비군국 민사과장)

       교통부장관 (관광국 관광진흥 과장)

       문화공보부장관 (해외공보관 외보 과장)

       보건사회부장관 (보건국 만성병과장, 약정국 마약과장)

0201-1-43A (2-2)　　　　　　　　　　190mm×265mm (2급인쇄용지 60g/m²)
1972. 12. 20 승 인　　　　　　　　　　도 단 성 (2,000,000에 인 쇄)

0004

공   란

공   란

공   란

보 건 사 회 부

만성 1433.4- 720ρ   (70-3711)   1976. 5. 3.

수신 외무부장관

참조 북미 2 과장

제목 SOFA 문민관계 임시분과 위원회 미군 기지촌 시찰

　　1. 미이 723-9537 (76. 4. 27)호와 관련임.

　　2. 대호에 의한 미군 기지촌 시찰계획에 당부로서는 만성병과장이

참석토록 되었음을 알리오니 양지하시기 바랍니다. 끝.

보 건 사 회 부

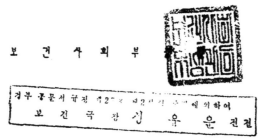

정부 공문서 규정 제2조 제2항의 규정에 의하여
보 건 국 장 신 유 운 전결

0008

SOFA 군민관기 위원티

기지촌 시찰 일정

1976. 5. 12. (수)
동두천 미 2시단 기지촌

09 : 00	중앙성 출발
10 : 30	미 제2시단 방문 및 브리핑
11 : 30 ~ 12 : 30	오 식 (미 2시단 영내)
13 : 00 ~ 13 : 40	동두천읍 브리핑
13 : 40 ~ 14 : 30	기지촌 시찰 (동두천읍장 안내)
14 : 30	서울 향발 (16:00 경 도착 예정)

8

0009

1976.

業 務 現 況

楊州郡 東豆川邑

0010

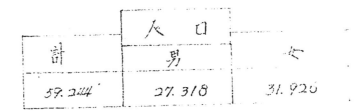

1 一般現況

面積	行政區域			
	法定里	行政里	自然部落	國民班
90.59 Km²	11	26	32	412

	人口	
計	男	女
59.244	27.318	31.920

	數口	
計	農家	非農家
12.797	1.335	11.462

0011

10

2. 綸落 女性 現況

總人員	登錄人員	未登錄人員	未登錄人員 內訳	
			美軍과 同棲	檢診忌避
名 2,700	2,172	528	250	278

3. 觀光業所 現況

區 分	業所數	從業員數	收容能力	備 考
計	25	316	2,900	
釜山地區	18	234	2,100	
廣告地區	7	82	800	

0046 0008 0012

ㅇ 性病對策

　1) 性病診療所 （2個所）✔

　　가 備落女性으로 하여금 週2回 定期的으로 檢診케 하여 落檢者는 性病管理所로 移送 完治后 退院 措置

　　나 隨時 街頭檢問을 實施 및 布이 ...者는 檢診后 收容治療하고 性病의 없는者는 登錄시킨后 歸家措置하고있음

　　다 診療對策

　　　　機構: 醫師　　2名
　　　　　　　看護員　3
　　　　　　　病理士　3
　　　　　　　行政　　2
　　　　　　　染色士　1
　　　　　　　計　　11

　　라 實績(76年) 受檢者 並 42,385名
　　　　　　　　　落檢者　1,234 · (3%)

0013

2) 性病管理所

收容能力　　200名

現在收容人員　40"

內容

◎ 落檢된 倫落女性을 入院 治療 后

退院 措置

◎ 治療費 負擔

治療費 및 食代一切 無料 施以

機構

醫　師　　2名

看護員　　3"

病理士　　3"

行政職　　2"

1975年度 治療実績

淋疾　　1,114名

梅毒　　120"

計　　1,234"

3) 職業輔導院院

  收容能力: 80 名

  現收容人員: 60 〃

 保健所 婦女相談員 警察官 合同 團束

 未成年者 及 無籍 家出 女性 職業訓練

5. 韓美親善 事業

 1) 韓美親善會議

  가. 構成者

   韓 國: {代議員

     邑長 支署長 邑諮問委員長 外 四人

   美 國: 支援司令官, 民事參謀, 憲兵參謀

    醫務參謀 外 3人

  나. 會期: 年 12回. 韓國: 6回. 美國: 6回

  다. 主要解決事項

   커뮤 事業 設備 支援

   性病管理에 對한 相互 協助

   美 2 師團 周邊 保山里 家基 6 棟 撤去

    棟當 40 萬원 補助 投住

0015

2) 親善体育大會
　　　開催狀況 : 年 2 回 (春秋)
　　　競技種目 : 蹴球
　　　　　　　主要人事 오락께임

3) 産業 및 觀光視察
　　　資格 : 歸國予定인 美國軍人
　　　　　　就任한 美軍軍人

　　視察地 :
　　　　産業視察地 : 2 個所 (울양카면 삼강스포쯔)
　　　　觀光地 : 1 個所 (춤꾸능)

15

0046 0008 00 16

其他: 韓食으로 夕食 待接
　　　年 6回 實施
　　　記念品 (패) 贈呈

#) 韓美交情事業
　　事業內容 ㉠ 韓國家庭에 美軍을 招請하여
　　　　　　　風俗과 生活相을 紹介 하며
　　　　　　　韓美 親善 强化
　　　　　 ㉡ 韓食接待로 韓食味 提高
　　　　　 ㉢ 年中事業으로 實施
　　韓國家庭에 招待 韓國에 주둔하고있는
　　美軍의 勞苦를 慰勞

0017

6. 基地料 淨化 事業

　1） 1995年度 議政府, 東豆川間 平和路工事 및
　　 12億円을 投資 開發 하였으며 東豆川 淨化
　　 事業 內容은 아래와 같습니다

事 業 名	單位	數 量	備 考
淸潔 아파트	棟	350	
住宅 改良	″	335	
自主化同商街 아파트	″	20	
住宅 撤去	″	79	
放送遊物 整備	″	350	
遊物 工事	″	1130	
撤去家屋	″	317	
看板整備	個所	458	
公營線 鋪裝	m a	2,000	450
道路入口 鋪裝	m a	1700	452
흇핀곡 ″	個所 m a	4	242
쓰레기 設置	個所 m	5	2430
側溝 整備	個所 m	11	1288
進 入路鋪裝	個所 a	33	46

0018

7. 連鎖商街 開設 計劃

規格: 一式

事業名 區分	事業量	事業費	備考
計	10,300㎡	346,100	
工場 敷地 造成	3,300	79,600	
公設 運動場 設置	5,000	229,400	
市場 開設	1,500	87,500	
貨物車 駐車場 施設	500	10,500	

8. 上水道施設 擴張 計劃

事業名	事業量	事業費	76年	77年	78年
計		148,000	65,000	63,000	20,000
여과지	2지	40,000	40,000		
배수지	1지	25,000	25,000		
송주관	L=1.2㎞	18,000		18,000	
취개법	L=150m	45,000		45,000	
배수관	L=3.7㎞	20,000			20,000

0019

9. 建議事項

ㄱ) 美軍이 韓國에 勤務期間中 東豆川
地域 社會開發에 參與한 操縱非共
에게 邑長의 感謝牌 工申 機會 주어

ㄴ) 美陸軍 第二師團 營內 或은 營外에 韓國
館 과 公報館을 施設 하여 우리기타 의
文化와 藝術을 弘報 하도록 建議 要望

19

0020

한 국 특 수 관 광 휴 양 업 협 회

관휴협제 97호   1976. 5. 25.

수   신   SOFA 한미 합동위원회 한국측 위원장
제   목   건 의 서

        당협회 산하에 있는 관광휴양업소는 관광사업진흥법에 의해
관광휴양업의 등록및 외국인전용 관광사업의 지정(주한유엔군및 외국인선원
전용)을 받은 업소로서 210여개의 업소가 전국 기지촌및 항만 지역에 산재
하여 주한유엔군및 외국인선원에게 휴양처를 제공하고 있으며 정부에서 면
세주류를 공급받아 염가도 제공하고 좋은 환경조성과 최대한의 써비스로서 이
들의 사기앙양과 한미친선에 기여하고 있는바
미게 2사단 제 3여단 주둔지역인 경기도 파주지역에서는 미군당국에서 관광
휴양업소에 대하여 별첨내용과 같이 부당한 간섭내지는 행위를 자행하고 있
어 마음놓고 영업을 할수없으며 항상 미군당국의 기배하에 인권을 유린당하
고 있어 이의 시정을 건의하오니 선처하여 주시옵기 바라나이다.

첨   부   1. 낙원크럽 미군출입금지 조치 공문 사본   1 부
             2. 진 술 서   3 부
             3. 업소또는 거리에 부친 미군출입금지 표시 사진등   4 매
             4. 서부지역 크럽 고객을 위한 종합규준 사본   1 부   끝.

                     한 국 특 수 관 광 휴 양 업 협 회
                     회 장   이   건

0021

공   란

공 란

공 란

공란

공   란

공   란

공   란

공 란

공   란

공　　　란

공   란

공　　란

공   란

공   란

공   란

공　　　란

공 란

공　　　　란

공   란

공   란

공 란

공　　　란

공   란

공   란

공 란

공   란

공　　　란

공 란

공   란

공   란

공　　　란

공   란

공   란

공   란

2

한 국 특 수 관 광 유 양 업 협 회

관유협제144호   1976. 7. 21.

수 신   한미협동위원회 한국측 위원장
제 목   건의사에 대한 변경상황보고

　　1. 관유협제 97호 (76. 5. 25)와 관련 사항입니다.
　　2. 미제 2사단 제 3여단장 경질 (76. 6. 1자)후 다음과 같이
상황이 변경 되었기 보고 합니다.

다

　　가. 파라다이스 그럽에 대한 미군출입 금지조처
　　　　문산읍 선유리 소재 파라다이스 그럽에 대한 미군 병사
들의 출입금지 조처는 76. 7. 1 제 3여단장 여단 민사참모 파주군 보건소장
합동으로 해업소를 검열후 당일로 해제 조치 하였음 (구두통지)

　　　　나. 관광유양업소에 대한 검열은 여단장 경질후로는 한미합동
으로 정거 검열만 실시하고 있음

　　　　다. 미군 기관에서 수시로 업소에 나와 영업실태를 점검하고
있으나 검열을 하는것이 아니고 영업상 잘못된 것을 시정요청하는 정도임

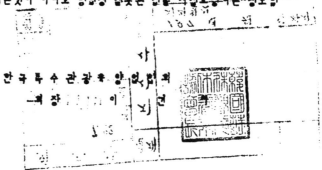

한 국 특 수 관 광 유 양 업 협 회
　　회 장   이

0056

정/리/보/존/문/서/목/록

기록물종류	문서-일반공문서철	등록번호	26010 9422	등록일자	2006-06-21
분류번호	729.419	국가코드		주제	
문서철명	SOFA 한.미국 합동위원회 군민관계 임시분과위원회, 제34차, 1976.7.23				
생산과	북미2과	생산년도	1976 ～ 1976	보존기간	영구
담당과(그룹)	미주	안보		서가번호	--
참조분류					
권차명					
내용목차					

마/이/크/로/필/름/사/항

촬영연도	★롤 번호	화일 번호	후레임 번호	보관함 번호
2006-11-29	G-06-0046	13	1-37	

0001

공   란

공   란

공   란

공   란

공   란

기 안 용 지

분류기호 문서번호	미이 723 -	(전화번호 70-2324)	전결규정 조항 전결사항 국장
처리기간			국 장
시행일자	1976. 7. 19.		
보존년한			

보조기관	심의관		협
	과 장		조
기안책임자	이창호	북미 2과	

경 유		
수 신	수신처 참조	
참 조		

제 목 : SOFA 제 34차 군민관계 임시분과위원회 개최통보

1976. 7. 19

검열 1976. 7. 19 통제과

1. 한.미 주둔군 지위협정(SOFA)의 제 34차 군민관계
임시분과위원회가 아래와 같이 개최되오니 위원께서는 필히 참석해
주시기 바랍니다.

- 아 래 -

가. 일 시 : 1976. 7. 23. 15:00

나. 장 소 : 미 8군 SOFA 회의실

다. 의 제 : 확정되는 대로 통보 위계임.

2. 제 33차 회의의 회의록을 별첨 송부하오니 참고하시기
바랍니다.

첨부 : 제 33차 군민관계 임시 분과위원회 회의록 각 1부. 끔.

0201-1-8A (갑)
1969. 11. 10 승 인

0007

190mm×268mm (2급인쇄용지60g/m²)
조 달 청 (1,000,000매 인쇄)

수신처 : 내무부 장관 (도시지도 과장)

　　　국방부 장관 (민사과장)

　　　보건사회부 장관 (만성병과장, 마약과장)

　　　고통부 장관 (관광진흥 과장)

　　　문학공보부 장관 (해외공보 과 외보 과장)

　　　법무부 장관 (송무 과장, 검찰 1 과장)

　　　내무부 장관 (외사과장, 수사지도 과장)

0008

공 란

공   란

공   란

공   란

공   란

공   란

공　　　란

공   란

공   란

공   란

공 란

공   란

공   란

공   란

공   란

공   란

공   란

미 2사단 지역 시찰 결과 보고서 요지

수 신 : 합동위원희

제 목 : 군민관기 임시분과위원희 제 21차 보고

1. 군민관기 임시분과위원희 위원 17명은 76. 5. 12.
   동두천 지역의 미 제 2사단 (캠프 케이시) 인근
   기지촌을 시찰하였는 바, 동 지역 시찰은 71. 9. 10.
   시찰 이래 4년만에 갖게 된 것임.
   시찰단은 미 2사단 및 동두천읍 이 마련한 브리핑을
   청취하였으며 미 2사단 사령부 에서 오찬을 가졌음.
   시찰단은 또한 양주군이 미군들에게 대여하고 있는
   주택 건물, 기지촌 소재유흥업소 및 소요산 성병
   치료소를 시찰하였음.

2. 시찰단을 맞은 "써만" 사단장의 간단한 환영사가
   있은 다음 브리핑을 시작하였으며, 브리핑 장고는
   민사처의 "심프손" 소령이었음.

0026

3. 캠프 케이시 입구에 이르는 도로 확장은 미 2사단과
   동 지역 한국정부 관리들간의 상호 지원과 이해의
   한 좋은 본보기로 지적되었는 바, 경기도와 한국 건설
   회사 요원들은 여러가지 문제점이 있었음에도 인내심을
   가지고 동 공사에 임했음. 또 하나의 좋은 예는 제 2
   항공대대의 수송부 개조 작업이었다고 심프슨 소령은
   설명하였음.

4. 이하에서 언급되고 있는 것은 미 2사단 및 동두천읍
   사무소에서 행한 브리핑에서 도출된 주요 문제점들임.

5. 문제점의 하나는 부대지역의 침식(encroachment)
   임. 동 브리핑에 의하면 경기도 지사는 이 문제의 해결을
   위해 역점을 두고 있음에도 불구하고 2사단으로서는
   아직까지도 문제점을 겪고 있다 함. 최근 다그 마트
   사격장 지역의 시찰 결과에 의하면 동 인근 지역에서
   미 2사단의 훈련 능력을 심히 제한하는 범위까지 미곡 및
   소맥을 경작하고 있는 것이 판명되었음. 또한 로드 비지스
   사격장 지역에서는 침식으로 말미암아 그 인근 지역의

0027

거의 절반이 사단 훈련에 저해가 되고 있음. 이러한
집식 문제에 관하여 경기도 와 군당국은 2사단 과의
협조 하에 이를 제거하기 위한 노력을 경주 하여 왔음.

6. 또 한가지 문제는 사단 인근 지역 상점에서 사단 장병
들에게 외상 거래를 하는 문제로서 이들 상점이 부과
하는 이자는 50% - 100%에 달하고 있는 바, 외상대금을
받지 못할 경우 자주는 사단 본부가 조력해 줄 것을
요청하는 경우 가 때때로 있다고 함. 또한 전당포 에서는
현금 대신 무 관세 물품등을 요구할 때도 있어서 사단에
대한 행정적인 부담이 될 뿐만 아니라 한국의 법병에도
위배되고 있음.

7. 군 부대에서의 미 정부 재산 도난도 우려되는 문제의
하나가 되고 있음. 도난 사례가 최근 감소 되고 있음은
다행한 일임. 간혹, 미 장병들이 도난에 관계되는 점도
있어 이들에 대한 적절한 인사 조치를 계속 취하고 있음.

8. 한국 관리들의 단호한 노력 결과, 사단 지역에서의
일반 약품 매매 문제는 그리 중요한 문제로 대두되지는
않으나 마비학나 및 대마초의 밀매와 사용은 만연되고

0028

있음. 이러한 습관성 약품은 부대 인근 마을에서
쉽게 구입할 수 있는 것으로 판명되고 있으며, 이를
팔지 못하도록 통제하는 노력이 아쉬운 것 같음.

9. 차별 행위가 간혹 있어 문젯거리가 되고 있음.
그러나 한.미 관비들의 감독과 통제로 이 문제는 점차
완화되고 있음.

10. 사단이나 인근지역의 본 문젯거리가 되고 있는 것은
성병 감염율 임. 감염율은 무서운 비율로 계속되고
있는 바, 통계에 의하면 76년도에 들어와서는 월간
1,200 ~ 1,800 건의 감염율을 보여주고 있음. 동두천
지역의 위안부 수는 2,700여명에 이르고 있는데 이중
약 500명이 등록되지 않은 채로 있음. 사단과 동두천읍
간에는 성병 문제가 해결 방안을 강구하기 위한 긴밀한
협조가 유지되고 있는데, 현재까지 취해진 조치는
미등록 위안부 및 매주 2회의 검진을 받지 않은 자들의
색출, 미 2사단의 중점적 조기 성병 교육, 사단지역 위안부
에 대한 성병교육 실시, 위안부들로 하여금 새로운 직업을
선택할 수 있기 위한 직업 훈련 제공등의 조치가 있었음.

0029

또한 성병을 진단하기 위한 배양 검사의 필요성이
강조되었음. 미2사단은 재감염 가능성과 지속적인
만연을 감소하기 위해 강경한 조치를 취하고 있음.

11. 양측 브리핑에서는 한.미 우호 협력 및 People to People
불법의 참여를 통한 상호 협조 와 이익을 검토하였음.

12. 상기에서 언급된 문제 해결 노력의 일환으로서 군민
관계 임시 분과위원회는 다음과 같은 조치를 취하기로
함.

가. 임시 분과위원회의 지역사회 및 정부간 관계
실무반과 한국 경찰, 미국 헌병간의 협력 및
조정에 관한 실무반의 양측 위원들은 미군장병
들과 동지역 상점들 간의 외상 매매 또는 무관세
및 군용물품의 고한 실태에 대한 상황을 조사하여
이러한 상황을 제거하기 위하여 취해야 할 적절한
조치를 결정한 후 60일 이내에 군민관계 임시분과
위원회에 동 결과를 보고하도록 함. 또한 제2사단
지역내의 도난 사고에 대한 문제도 아울러 조사토록
함.

0030

나. 미측은 부대지역 침식 문제의 처리를 위한
적절한 협조 체계를 강구하도록 하고 이러한
체계를 통하여 적절한 결과가 이루어지지 않을
경우에는 이를 임시 분과위원회에 넘겨 토의도록
함.

다. 보건 위생 실무반은 2사단 지역내의 성병문제를
조사하고 높은 성병 감염율을 감소시키기 위하여
취해야 할 적절한 조치를 결정, 동 결과를 60일
이내에 임시 분과위원회에 보고하도록 함.

라. 마약 단속 실무반은 2사단 지역에서의 마리확나
및 대마초의 밀매 상황을 면밀히 감시하고 주 간격
으로 취해야 할 조치의 필요성을 판단하여 60일
이내에 군민관계 임시분과위원회에 보고도록 함.

- 끝 -

0031

공　　　란

공   란

공   란

공 란

공　　란

공   란

외교문서 비밀해제: 주한미군지위협정(SOFA) 40

주한미군지위협정(SOFA) 군민관계 임시분과위원회 5

초판인쇄 2024년 03월 15일
초판발행 2024년 03월 15일

지은이 한국학술정보(주)
펴낸이 채종준
펴낸곳 한국학술정보(주)
주 소 경기도 파주시 회동길 230(문발동)
전 화 031-908-3181(대표)
팩 스 031-908-3189
홈페이지 http://ebook.kstudy.com
E-mail 출판사업부 publish@kstudy.com
등 록 제일산-115호(2000. 6. 19)

ISBN 979-11-7217-051-6 94340
       979-11-7217-011-0 94340 (set)